✦ Praise for Emotionally Intelligent Leadership for Students: Development Guide

"Current events have caused us to reconsider the CEO-worshipping of the past two decades, encouraging us to invest in the potential of college students—our next generation of leaders. Shankman and Allen provide an intriguing model for developing emotionally intelligent leaders who understand the complexities of and champion the cause for authentic human relationships, thriving organizations, and vibrant communities."

—Tom Matthews, director, Career Center,
Case Western Reserve University

"Shankman and Allen have provided a strong theoretical framework on emotionally intelligent leadership and the student development guide is a perfect complement to their work. It is easy to understand and allows for students to work at their own pace in strengthening their EIL. The suggestions provided are relevant to today's students and enhance the work of leadership educators."

—Mallory Anderson, director, The Center for
Leadership, Elon University

"Students who master emotionally intelligent leadership while in college will find the skills transferable to all future professional and personal endeavors. *EIL for Students: Development Guide* is a one of a kind book which enables student leaders to have a variety of resources to develop their EIL."

—Allison St. Germain, director of educational
technologies, Delta Zeta

"Finally! Shankman and Allen have pulled together the very best resources for focused leadership development from diverse and exhaustive sources. This book is the epitome of one-stop shopping."

—Don DiPaolo, associate professor of education,
University of Detroit Mercy

"Simply put, Shankman and Allen's work equips students for the immense challenge of leadership. *EIL for Students: Development Guide* is chock-full of useful ideas that can be applied immediately to increase leadership effectiveness."

—Ed O'Malley, president and CEO,
Kansas Leadership Center

Emotionally Intelligent Leadership for Students

Development Guide

Marcy Levy Shankman & Scott J. Allen

JOSSEY-BASS™
STUDENT LEADERSHIP

The Jossey-Bass Higher and Adult Education Series

Published by Jossey-Bass
A Wiley Imprint
989 Market Street, San Francisco, CA 94103-1741—www.josseybass.com

Readers should be aware that Internet Web sites offered as citations and/or sources for further information may have changed or disappeared between the time this was written and when it is read.

Limit of Liability/Disclaimer of Warranty: While the publisher and author have used their best efforts in preparing this book, they make no representations or warranties with respect to the accuracy or completeness of the contents of this book and specifically disclaim any implied warranties of merchantability or fitness for a particular purpose. No warranty may be created or extended by sales representatives or written sales materials. The advice and strategies contained herein may not be suitable for your situation. You should consult with a professional where appropriate. Neither the publisher nor author shall be liable for any loss of profit or any other commercial damages, including but not limited to special, incidental, consequential, or other damages.

Jossey-Bass books and products are available through most bookstores. To contact Jossey-Bass directly call our Customer Care Department within the U.S. at 800-956-7739, outside the U.S. at 317-572-3986, or fax 317-572-4002.

Jossey-Bass also publishes its books in a variety of electronic formats. Some content that appears in print may not be available in electronic books.

Library of Congress Cataloging-in-Publication Data

Emotionally intelligent leadership for students : development guide / Marcy Levy Shankman and Scott J. Allen, editors.

    p. cm. — (The Jossey-Bass higher and adult education series)

  Includes bibliographical references.

  ISBN 978-0-470-61573-7 (pbk.)

  1. Educational leadership. 2. Teacher effectiveness. I. Shankman, Marcy Levy. II. Allen, Scott J., 1972-

LB2346.E47 2010

371.2001'9—dc22

2010009692

Printed in the United States of America

FIRST EDITION

PB Printing   10 9 8 7 6 5 4 3 2 1

CONTENTS

PREFACE

When we sat down to write the book *Emotionally Intelligent Leadership: A Guide for College Students*, we began by discussing the purpose of the book. Although some authors may come to a project with different goals, we came with a shared vision. We intended to write the book as a vehicle for sharing our ideas with as broad an audience as possible. We wanted to introduce emotionally intelligent leadership (EIL) to students, professionals working with students, faculty, and others who engage with students throughout their college experience.

Simply put, we believe this subject has the potential to make a difference in student leadership development. For students, EIL provides a lens to view themselves and enhance their capacity to make a difference on campus and in their community. For those working with students, EIL provides a framework for supervision, advising, teaching, mentoring, coaching—the application potential is wide open.

In some ways, we think about EIL as the baseball diamond in the movie *Field of Dreams*—"If you build it, they will come." Leadership is available to all of us—and to all students who desire to enhance their skills. Student organizations, residence halls, project teams, workplaces, the larger campus community—all are potential practice fields for those interested in making a difference in the lives of others. And we think EIL provides students with one way to embark on a future full of amazing possibilities.

So here we are, on the next step of our journey—and, we hope, of yours. From the outset, even while we were writing the book, we envisioned a suite of EIL resources. These resources provide direct, hands-on learning experiences for students and professionals alike. The suite consists of five separate but interrelated resources:

- *Emotionally Intelligent Leadership: A Guide for College Students*
- *Emotionally Intelligent Leadership for Students: Inventory*
- *Emotionally Intelligent Leadership for Students: Facilitation and Activity Guide*
- *Emotionally Intelligent Leadership for Students: Student Workbook*
- *Emotionally Intelligent Leadership for Students: Development Guide*

✦ Emotionally Intelligent Leadership: A Guide for College Students

Emotionally Intelligent Leadership: A Guide for College Students is a groundbreaking book that combines the concepts of emotional intelligence (EI) and leadership in one model: emotionally intelligent leadership (EIL). This important resource offers students a practical guide for developing their EIL capacities and emphasizes that leadership is a learnable skill that is based on developing healthy and effective relationships. Step by step, we outline the EIL model of three facets (consciousness of context, consciousness of self, and consciousness of others) and explore the twenty-one capacities that define emotionally intelligent leadership.

✦ The Inventory

One of the greatest challenges in leadership development is translating theory into practice—how do the big ideas about leadership make sense to us as individuals so that we can behave differently? Talking about leadership is one thing—integrating ideas about leadership into our thoughts and actions is another. Assessments serve many purposes along this line—making an abstract concept real, translating theory into practice, and finding meaningful connections between ideas and ourselves. The *Inventory* is our contribution to the field of assessment.

The *Inventory* offers a formative learning experience. While some leadership assessments are diagnostic or predictive in nature, the *Inventory* is an opportunity for individuals to explore their experiences in leadership with a focus on learning one's strengths and limitations based on past behaviors. At the same time, the *Inventory* propels students' thinking into the future with a focus on self-improvement and leadership development. Results include an enhanced understanding of EIL and its application, identification of perceived strengths and limitations, and a determination of direction for leadership development.

✦ The Facilitation and Activity Guide

The *Facilitation and Activity Guide* is written for leadership educators and practitioners, campus-based professionals, faculty, and anyone interested in guiding students through hands-on learning opportunities that deepen their understanding of emotionally intelligent leadership. The *Facilitation and Activity Guide* is organized in a similar fashion to *Emotionally Intelligent Leadership: A Guide for College Students*, with at least one chapter (module) dedicated to each of the three facets (consciousness of context, consciousness of self, consciousness of others) and the twenty-one capacities of EIL. Each module provides everything that a facilitator needs to know to prepare and facilitate the learning experience (generally forty-five to sixty minutes in length). The modules are written with specific directions, talking points, and discussion questions. When supplemental materials are needed,

they are listed at the outset. This resource includes the worksheets, also found in the *Student Workbook,* that the students
may utilize during the course of the learning experience. Finally,
the *Facilitation and Activity Guide* includes a facilitation plan,
suggested program designs, and syllabi in the appendices.

✦ The Student Workbook

Recognizing the need for students to actively engage in their learning, the *Student Workbook* supports and complements the material
covered in the *Facilitation and Activity Guide* and the *Inventory.*
The *Student Workbook* includes handouts, learning activities, case
studies, questions for reflection, and additional resources for further
learning. Each chapter of the *Student Workbook* follows the flow
of *Emotionally Intelligent Leadership: A Guide for College Students*
and the *Facilitation and Activity Guide.* Students may also use the
Student Workbook as a follow-up to the *EIL Inventory.*

✦ The Development Guide

The *Development Guide* provides students with hundreds of ideas
for improvement. The *Development Guide* offers the reader a
description of each capacity and a picture of what it looks like to
others when an individual is over- or underusing each capacity.
In addition, we identify dozens of films, online resources, learning opportunities, books, student quotes, and reflection questions
for each of the twenty-one capacities. An individual interested
in developing these skills will find a strong foundation in the
material and the guidance needed to begin this work.

Eleanor Roosevelt said "living and learning go hand in
hand" (Gerber, 2002, p. 256). We believe that this notion

extends to leadership—we all have the potential to lead. It's up to us to do it. We hope these resources help students further discover the leadership potential within them. And we hope these materials empower those working with students—to help them guide students in their development, and perhaps, along the way, learn more about their own leadership. We certainly have.

Marcy Levy Shankman, Ph.D.
Scott J. Allen, Ph.D.

REFERENCE

Gerber, R. (2002). *Leadership the Eleanor Roosevelt way: Timeless strategies from the first lady of courage*. New York: Portfolio.

ACKNOWLEDGMENTS

We are indebted to our wonderful editor, Erin Null. She has been an important partner in developing these materials with guidance and continued enthusiasm. Each time we bring a creative (or crazy) idea to her, she responds with clarity and thoughtfulness.

Finally, we are thankful that we both have families that are patient and always supportive—they keep us grounded and remind us of why we do the work that we do.

ABOUT THE AUTHORS

Marcy Levy Shankman, Ph.D., has been training and consulting in leadership development and organizational effectiveness since 1998. She is principal of MLS Consulting LLC, which she founded in 2001. Marcy works with a wide range of clients, from small direct service agencies to national voluntary associations, from local high schools to large public universities. Marcy facilitates strategic planning and visioning initiatives, organizational change and development projects, as well as leadership training and board development. Marcy has spoken to various groups in the local nonprofit community as well as conferences and campuses across the country. Her focus is on helping students, young and experienced professionals, faculty, and staff consider ways to enhance their own leadership development.

Marcy also teaches as a Presidential Fellow for the SAGES program at Case Western Reserve University and as an instructor in the David Brain Leadership Program of Baldwin-Wallace College. Prior to establishing her training and consulting practice, Marcy held professional positions with the Indiana University Center on Philanthropy, the Hillel Foundation at the George Washington University, and the Office of Orientation Services at the University of Iowa.

Marcy actively volunteers with her alma mater, The College of William and Mary, her local school district, the learning committee of her synagogue, and the Organizational Assessment Committee of the United Way of Greater Cleveland.

Marcy lives in Shaker Heights, Ohio, with her husband and two children.

Scott J. Allen, Ph.D., is an assistant professor of management at John Carroll University, where he teaches leadership and management skills. In 2005, Scott developed the Center for Leader Development (www.centerforleaderdevelopment.com), a blog that explores the study and practice of leadership development.

Scott is published in the *Encyclopedia of Leadership* and completed a chapter for the China Executive Leadership Academy Pudong, entitled "A Review on Leadership Education and Development Outside China." He is also a contributing author of the book *Leadership: The Key Concepts* (Routledge, 2007). In addition, his work is featured in a number of academic journals, such as the *Journal of Leadership Educators*, *Advances in Developing Human Resources*, *Leadership Review*, *The OD Journal*, *SAM Advanced Management Journal*, *International Leadership Journal*, *Journal of Leadership Studies*, and *Leadership Excellence.*

In addition to his writing and work in the classroom, Scott consults, facilitates workshops, and leads retreats across industries. Scott is involved in the International Leadership Association and serves on the board of trustees of Beta Theta Pi Fraternity. Since 2007, he has served as a Sam Walton Fellow for Students in Free Enterprise (SIFE).

Scott resides in Chagrin Falls, Ohio, with his wife and three children.

DEVELOPING EMOTIONALLY INTELLIGENT LEADERSHIP

Developing leadership capacity is a difficult process. In this short opening section we share some thoughts on getting started. There is no set recipe or formula that works for everyone, so we are going to share a number of different ideas, hoping that some will resonate with you. We will move back and forth from general theories about learning to simple, straightforward ideas that you can implement today. Regardless, know that developing emotionally intelligent leadership (EIL) is a long-term endeavor. Like any other knowledge, skill, or ability, it takes years to develop mastery.

Here are a few general suggestions for beginning or continuing your leadership development.

First, let a mentor or friend know that you want to improve. By doing so, you will invite them to help you, and they can hold you accountable. Sharing with others that you want to improve can be challenging, because it places you in a vulnerable position. However, when others know you're trying to develop and grow, they tend to be more understanding of mistakes and perhaps more interested in helping you learn. Think about how athletes or musicians place themselves in the same position. To excel and develop their skills, they must practice and be open to feedback from their coach. Many would agree that LeBron James has incredible natural ability, but he needed people like his mother and others along the way to guide him to the next level. Who is guiding you?

Second, we suggest placing yourself in environments in which you can practice the capacities you hope to develop. We call these *edge* experiences. You know you are at your *edge* when you have a nervous feeling in your stomach—a feeling of uncertainty as to how things will turn out. For some, this may be public speaking; for others, it may be leading a high visibility project. Being at the edge requires some risk taking. What is your edge? What experiences will take your abilities to a new level? Who can help you along the way? Clarity about these questions is paramount as you strive to develop your leadership abilities.

Of utmost importance is *intentionality*. Effective leadership takes commitment and awareness. In other words, just as with any other skill or ability, you have to *want* to develop your leadership abilities. This requires changes in behavior. Effective leadership takes practice—and if you want to improve your knowledge, skills, and abilities, you must take the time and devote your attention to the process.

Think about leadership development as a learning process. To develop or learn a skill (such as cooking, effective listening, public speaking, dancing, lacrosse, and so forth), we each go through the *four stages of competence* (see a table depicting the "conscious competence" learning model at http://www.businessballs.com/consciouscompetencelearning model.htm). These are the four stages:

- *Unconscious incompetence*—the person is not aware of the existence or relevance of the skill area
- *Conscious incompetence*—the person becomes aware of the existence and relevance of the skill
- *Conscious competence*—the person achieves "conscious competence" in a skill when he or she can perform it reliably at will
- *Unconscious competence*—the skill becomes so practiced that it enters the unconscious parts of the brain; that is, it becomes "second nature"

Now reread the four stages and consider the following example:

Think about a professional figure skater. In the beginning she does not know what she does not know—she is oblivious to all aspects of what it means to be a skilled figure skater (unconscious incompetence).

After a while, she begins to become aware of what she needs to do to be proficient as a skater, and she becomes aware of her many limitations (consciousness incompetence). If she immerses herself in a skating environment and spends time working with a coach to develop her skills, she can improve, with focused determination and practice (conscious competence). With practice and experience, many of the initial challenges fade into the background, and the initial struggles no longer take conscious thought. She no longer needs to think about the basics of skating (unconscious competence). Of course, as she takes her knowledge, skills, or abilities to the next level, she will go through the same process again.

This example demonstrates what anyone goes through in learning how to demonstrate a talent or skill—be they a LeBron James, a Serena Williams, a Tony Hawk, a Beyoncé, a Shaun White, or one of the rest of us who are not so famous.

← Levels of Leadership Learning

So how can you intentionally move through this process as it relates to developing emotionally intelligent leadership? The following suggestions provide a roadmap.

Level One: Knowledge and Awareness

To develop any skill or ability, even if it doesn't relate to leadership development, you must possess certain knowledge. For instance, to earn a black belt in karate requires multiple levels of knowledge about the techniques, rules, regulations, and overall language of the sport. To an untrained eye, however, this knowledge is unseen. We see only the abilities or skills that the person demonstrates. If you take the time to understand the inner workings of what is happening (the techniques, rules, and so on), you can better understand them.

In other words, you must acquire the knowledge to appreciate the complexities and dynamics of the sport.

Applying this process to leadership, then, you need to conceptually understand leadership as the first step in the process of development. For instance, you should have an understanding of various leadership theories and styles (such as transformational leadership, relational leadership, shared leadership), emotional intelligence, power dynamics, influence strategies, communication (such as nonverbal and small group), facilitating change, motivating others, management theory, and so forth. A conceptual understanding is only the beginning.

Unfortunately, it is here that most leadership training or development programs end. However, to intentionally develop EIL, you need to know and do more.

Level Two: Observation

Observation is the second level; this is where conceptual knowledge and understanding move into action. The information is no longer simply resting unused in your brain. When you observe, you are applying your understanding through critical thinking. This is what helps inform your understanding of what is happening in your environment. An example can be found in the game of chess. Once a person understands the fundamentals of chess, she can begin to see the strategy of the game in real time. As she watches the game, she can anticipate the next move or envision the consequences of a move just taken. She is no longer just an uninformed observer watching a number of pieces moving around randomly. She understands what is happening (and can name it).

Regarding leadership, when you're at this level of knowing, you can see (and name) an individual using a coercive style of leadership and the benefits and drawbacks of that approach. When you see someone overusing the capacity of optimism, you can see the impact that this has on her, as well as on the others with whom she is interacting. The EIL model forms a lens through which you can view successful or not-so-successful leadership. And as you observe different examples of leadership, you integrate these observations with your Level One knowledge to deepen your understanding.

Level Three: Scenario Planning

Based on sound knowledge and a keen awareness of what is occurring in the environment, the next level of learning entails brainstorming potential options in real time. For a chef, this thinking must happen in a matter of seconds or the dish could be ruined. Brainstorming options based on data in the environment is a skill that any master of a trade possesses. In the world of politics, an astute observer will be able to suggest the options at the political operative's disposal. Likewise, a seasoned psychologist will make a quick decision based on new data presented by her client.

Leadership is no different. Based on knowledge and awareness of the environment, the leader makes an informed decision (often a best guess) and prepares for action. This requires the emotionally intelligent leader to constantly be conscious of context, self, and others. By doing so, the leader is better prepared to choose from a list of options that will be suited to the current situation. Is this difficult to do successfully? Yes. However, as we've mentioned, any master of a trade moves through a similar process.

Level Four: Leader Intervention

Perhaps the most difficult aspect of leadership is the necessary intervention. At this stage, you work to help move the group or an idea forward. Based on sound knowledge of the topic, an observation of the context, and a well-designed plan, you must use your skills and ideas to act. Because this is a totally new level of mastery, you proceed with intentionality and an appreciation of the risk. You are not necessarily sure of the results, only of the plan and the ideas that support the plan. For example, a political analyst may perform on the first three levels with great success; however, this does not mean that the analyst has the ability to actually "do politics." Another example is a coach in athletics. In many instances this person does not have the abilities that those on the field do—perhaps he or she did at one time, but it is likely this person is coaching players with a higher level of skill than the coach (think Phil Jackson). The leader's tools are based on how he uses his own skills in working with others. To mobilize both, the leader needs to intervene with a high level of success.

Keep these levels of leadership learning in mind as you develop and hone your capacities. By doing so, you will be more intentional about your development. You will have a roadmap and guidelines to help you along the way. Too many people do not take the time to master all four levels—and it shows. Returning to the cooking example, ineffective leadership feels like eating poorly made meals, day after day after day. What kind of meals are you "cooking" for others? Four star? One star?

Ten Concrete Ways to Develop Any EIL Capacity—Today

1. *Locate and meet with a mentor who exemplifies the capacity.* Seek out a well-respected leader such as a professor or coach. The relationship does not have to be long term—it may simply consist of a couple of lunches or conversations in which you learn more about the individual's

perspective on the topic and what they did to master that capacity.

2. *Read an article or book on the capacity.* A book or article is a perfect way to learn more about the capacity. Plenty of research has been conducted on each of them, and the more you know (Level One knowledge), the better prepared you are to work on Levels Two through Four.

3. *Join a student organization or place yourself in situations that require you to practice the capacity.* As we mention in our book *Emotionally Intelligent Leadership: A Guide for College Students,* we feel that college provides a wonderful "practice field" for learning about leadership. Joining an organization and taking on a formal or informal leadership role is a great way to get to know, observe, plan, and exercise any leadership capacity.

4. *Take part in formal learning opportunities, retreats, or courses that focus on the capacity.* It is likely that you can find courses on campus touching on topics such as team development, small group communication, counseling psychology, and leadership. By learning about the capacity from an academic perspective, you are better prepared to put the theory into practice.

5. *Blog or journal about the process of developing the capacity.* Writing and reflecting on your experience is an important part of the learning process. The key is to reflect, in your writing, on the capacity you hope to develop. Think about it the next time you exercise. Talk about it with a friend as you walk to class. What system(s) can you put in place to help you remember that this capacity is your focus? It may be as simple as writing the capacity on the top of your agenda, or putting a sticky note on your mirror or in your planner.

6. *Have coffee or otherwise connect with others working on the same capacity and talk about your experience(s).* As with the preceding suggestion, you may need to get creative. But there's no

denying you will have a better chance of success in mastering a capacity if you collaborate with others in the effort. We understand that there probably is not an "EIL self-help group" on campus, but there are people you could connect with who likely struggle with the same capacity.

7. *Write a vision statement or story about a future positive state as it relates to the capacity.* Visualizing a future state can be a powerful tool; simply ask any high-performing artist or athlete. So what do you see? What will change as you master this capacity? How will that benefit you? How will others perceive you and how will that help you when leading others? We like the way author and futurist Joel Barker (1991) puts it: "Vision without action is merely a dream. Action without vision just passes time. Vision with action changes the world."

8. *Participate in opportunities to teach others about the capacity.* At first blush this may seem unrealistic, but when you think about it, you'll realize that opportunities to teach others are all around you. This may be a class presentation, group project, service-learning project, mentoring opportunity, or tutoring. Talk with others about what you are learning and why it is important. Years ago Confucius suggested, "What I hear I forget. What I see I remember. What I do I understand." Teaching is the highest form of learning.

9. *Complete an assessment or instrument that can help you learn more about your personality.* The career center and, most likely, the counseling center on your campus have numerous resources and assessments to assist you in developing your self-awareness. Take some time to investigate what's available, and consider going to the library to see what they may have. Assessments like the *EILS: Inventory*, the DISC, StrengthsFinder, Myers-Briggs Type Indicator (MBTI), or Strong Interest Inventory are good places to start.

10. *Find an internship that will require you to use (and practice) the capacity.* What internships will challenge you to use and develop emotionally intelligent leadership on a consistent basis? For instance, serving as a coach, camp counselor, tutor, or mentor will force you to demonstrate your leadership and develop any number of capacities on a consistent basis.

✦ Using the Development Guide

This *Development Guide* is designed to meet you where you are. You do not need to read it from start to finish. We suggest focusing on no more than one capacity at a time. This will give you space to move through the learning processes just described and get you off on the right foot. Take a couple of the ideas in this section (find a mentor and join a group) and read the section on the capacity you hope to develop. Investigate the resources we recommend and slowly begin to devise a plan for development. Through careful, thoughtful, deliberate action, and ongoing reflection, you will bring about intentional change and develop your knowledge, skills, and abilities.

REFERENCE

Barker, J. (1991). *The power of vision* (VHS). United States: Starthrower Distribution.

CAPACITY 1

Environmental Awareness

✦ Environmental Awareness Defined

In the *American Heritage Dictionary, environment* is defined as the complex of social and cultural conditions affecting the nature of an individual or community.

The larger system, or environment, directly influences an individual's ability to lead. Aspects of the environment affect the psychological and interpersonal dynamics of any human interaction. Emotionally intelligent leaders are in tune with a variety of factors such as community traditions and customs, the political environment, and major institutions (e.g., religion, government). Demonstrating environmental awareness means having the ability to observe these dynamics and factors present in the environment as they occur. Being aware of one's environment enables a person to use that knowledge to determine a course of action with greater perspective and insight.

Developing environmental awareness can be difficult. It is a skill that must be practiced intentionally. Why? It is simply human nature to react to stimuli rather than consciously observe. We also tend to focus only on ourselves: what is happening to us or what might influence us. Learning how to take a step back and observe what is going on around us comes with experience. Environmental awareness includes noticing the influences from outside the group or the situation that affect how people interact—for instance, how a group approaches its work during a high-stress time versus when the group first comes together after a successful event. Leaders who are aware of their environment use that knowledge to determine a course of action as well as anticipate potential challenges.

Too Much Environmental Awareness

Individuals focused too much on environmental awareness may get lost in the many dimensions of the environment and find themselves stuck in a labyrinth of possibilities. In other words, it is easy to become so focused on the larger system that little action occurs. Too much attention to the environment may translate into spending too much time think-ing about the external influences and subsequent hypothetical situations (the "what ifs"), instead of paying attention to what is happening in reality. In essence, a person can become immobilized by analyzing the external forces (real and potential) at play. This focus may take the person away from interacting with others or attending to responsibilities. As such, a leader too focused on this capacity may be perceived by others as being in the clouds and unable to make things happen on the ground and in real time.

Too Little Environmental Awareness

People with low levels of environmental awareness may find themselves blindsided by external factors that were previously invisible to them. In essence, a person who does not see the whole picture may make decisions that do not mesh with the broader reality of the situation. Opportunities may be lost or distorted because of the person's narrow perspective. This person also may not understand the dynamics of the group because of not noticing the impact of external forces. In addition, a leader with a low level of environmental awareness may lose sight of the organization's alignment with its intended purpose and its place in the larger community. How the organization links to the larger community is an important element that will affect the leader's ability to be successful.

Student Quotes

An environment that I feel comfortable in is a huge factor in my ability to lead. If I feel that I am in the kind of place where I can say what I want and take charge, then I am more likely to lead. However, if a teacher, advisor, or another student is imposing or not inviting, I often have the feeling that I want to just sit back and not be noticed.

The environment has everything to do with one's ability to lead. Everyone has a leadership style which comes naturally. Each style has positives and negatives. If the environment requires a leadership style not mastered by the leader, it becomes difficult to impact what goes on.

[The] environment can either make or break leadership ability. If you are working with others in an environment where they fully support your duties, you will succeed many times over.

If you are constantly battling for credibility, it will start to feel troublesome or hopeless.

After this past summer, environment has a new meaning to me. If an environment has an established culture, it is harder to get adjusted and bring the people along with you. In an office, the environment describes the mood, almost to what I want to call the "integrity" of the company. If it's a positive environment, that's great, but when it lacks support and communication, there is room for error and even failure.

❧ Online Articles and Resources

- http://managementhelp.org—Organizational Culture
- http://dayton.bizjournals.com—Strong culture can be a "double-edged sword"
- http://www.ericdigests.org—Organizational Culture and Institutional Transformation
- http://www.iproconhcm.co.uk/—What Is Organisational Culture and How Can You Change It?
- http://www.au.af.mil/au/—Organizational Culture

❧ Suggested Books

- *Group Dynamics* by Donelson R. Forsyth
- *Leadership on the Line* by Martin Linsky and Ronald A. Heifetz
- *Leadership Without Easy Answers* by Ronald A. Heifetz
- *Leadership Can Be Taught* by Sharon Daloz Parks
- *Organizational Culture and Leadership* by Edgar H. Schein

- *Reframing Organizations: Artistry, Choice, and Leadership* by Lee Bolman and Terrence Deal
- *How the Mighty Fall and Why Some Companies Never Give Up* by Jim Collins

⬳ Suggested Films

The following films highlight the capacity of environmental awareness. Some characters may overuse this capacity; others may lack the ability to use it successfully.

- *Primary Colors*
- *Wall Street*
- *Avatar*
- *Milk*
- *Norma Rae*
- *North Country*
- *Boiler Room*
- *The Smartest Guys in the Room*
- *Remember the Titans*
- *A League of Their Own*
- *Harry Potter* series
- *Gandhi*

⬳ Potential Courses That Relate to This Capacity

- *Cultural anthropology courses*
- *Business courses*—organizational behavior, leadership or management skills
- *Communication courses*—interpersonal communication, small group communications

- *Leadership courses*
- *Psychology courses*—small group dynamics, social psychology, organizational psychology, identity development
- *Sociology courses*—organizations, social institutions, community

← Notable Quotes

I will argue that the term "culture" should be reserved for the deeper level of basic assumptions and beliefs that are shared by members of an organization, that operate unconsciously, and that define in a basic "taken for granted" fashion an organization's view of itself and its environment.—Edgar Schein, author, *Organizational Culture and Leadership*

In order to understand people, we have to understand their way of life and approach. If we wish to convince them, we have to use their language in the narrow sense of the mind. Something that goes even much further than that is not the appeal to logic and reason, but some kind of emotional awareness of the other people.—Nehru, Indian statesman

Culture hides more than it reveals and strangely enough what it hides, it hides most effectively from its own participants. Years of study have convinced me that the real job is not to understand foreign culture but to understand our own.—Edward T. Hall, anthropologist

✦ Reflection Questions

Think about an organization or group that you are a part of:

- Is the organization doing a good job of doing what it is intended to do? Are its activities and mission (reason for existence) consistent with each other? How do you know this is true?
- How is the organization known by others outside of this group? How do you know this?
- How would you describe the level of acceptance from the campus or school community?
- What are the external challenges facing the group? Are there forces from outside the group that are helpful to the group? If so, what are they? If not, what would benefit the group?
- Is the organization seen as a benefit or detriment to the community? Explain.

CAPACITY 2

Group Savvy

✦ Group Savvy Defined

In the *American Heritage Dictionary*, *savvy* is defined as well informed and perceptive. To this term, add the word *group*: an assemblage of persons or objects gathered or located together; an aggregation.

Group savvy is about interpreting the situation and/or networks of an organization. Every group has written and unwritten rules, ways of operating, customs and rituals, power dynamics, internal politics, inherent values, and so forth. Emotionally intelligent leaders know how to diagnose and interpret these dynamics. Demonstrating group savvy enables one to have a direct influence on the work of the group. Group savvy helps a leader diagnose what is happening and how to accomplish the group's goals. Sometimes these elements are known and obvious—who is in charge by title or position, the written rules of the group, and so on. Often, though, as you dig deeper or spend more time in a group, you learn that the group operates differently from how you first thought it did. You learn who is actually in charge. You discover what really matters most to the group. You may even see who forms the in-group and who the outsiders are. When you demonstrate the capacity of group savvy, you ask questions to discover these answers, and often you learn more than you thought you knew about your group.

← Too Much Group Savvy

Individuals who are too focused on group savvy may get lost in the many layers of the organization and find themselves overwhelmed by the complexities and inner workings of the group. In other words, a person may become so engrossed with the internal group dynamics that little action occurs. When this happens, the leader can become paralyzed. In addition, a person too focused on this capacity may be perceived by others as overly political. When a person's attention is primarily focused on what's occurring within the group, who is seeking power, who is disengaged, and so on, then group members may think the person is more interested in the individuals, their personal issues, and their stories than in the goals of the group or furthering the group's mission.

← Too Little Group Savvy

Individuals with low levels of group savvy may find themselves blindsided by organizational issues and dynamics that were previously invisible to them. Disagreements among individuals, internal politics or plays on power, and other group dynamics may bubble to the surface without being recognized by this person. This can negatively affect the person's ability to help the work of the group move forward. Moreover, the person may miss seemingly obvious dynamics such as well-established group norms, values, and unwritten rules guiding the behaviors of members. Because a leader often helps shape group norms and values, if too little group savvy is being demonstrated, then the leader's influence is diminished.

✦ Student Quotes

When I'm first joining an organization, I always limit my active participation. Instead, I spend a lot of time watching the body language of long-time members. I notice (1) their manner of interaction with each other and (2) their reaction to other newcomers in the group. From these interactions, I infer social norms. Following the internal rules of the organization lets me get what I want out of the organization. For example, I have to act brashly in my college residence hall if I want anyone to notice me, but that sort of attitude would have gotten me fired from my summer internship.

Clearly, the easiest way to learn the unwritten rules or internal workings of an organization is to be fully engulfed in the organization. By carefully listening and evaluating an organization an individual can quickly (this being a very relative term) discover the internal workings and organizational culture that exist within an organization.

Someone learns the unwritten rules, by either learning from example or by actually being told by a member with more experience. A new student may learn the unwritten rules by asking an older more seasoned member of the group. Or the new person may learn by observing what is done and what is not done.

Such knowledge of an organization comes with being active in the group for a period of time. The process is expedited if you have a leadership role and actually help create the plans for the group.

Online Articles and Resources

- http://www.grouprelations.com—Group Relations Theory
- http://www.wilderdom.com—Group Dynamics, Process and Development
- http://ksgexecprogram.harvard.edu—The Art and Practice of Leadership Development
- http://www.tavinstitute.org—Tavistock Institute

Suggested Books

- *Hot Groups* by Jean Lipman-Blumen and Harold J. Leavitt
- *Group Dynamics* by Donelson R. Forsyth
- *Leadership on the Line* by Martin Linsky and Ronald A. Heifetz
- *Leadership Without Easy Answers* by Ronald A. Heifetz
- *Leadership Can Be Taught* by Sharon Daloz Parks
- *Organizational Culture in Action: A Cultural Analysis Workbook* by Gerald Driskill and Angela Laird Brenton
- *In Good Company: How Social Capital Makes Organizations Work* by Don Coehn and Laurence Prusak

✦ Suggested Films

The following films highlight the capacity of group savvy. Some characters may overuse this capacity; others may lack the ability to use it successfully.

- *The Big Chill*
- *City Slickers*
- *The Lord of the Rings* trilogy
- *Star Wars* series
- *Steel Magnolias*
- *Ocean's 11*
- *Shrek*
- *Apollo 13*
- *Thirteen Days*
- *Dances with Wolves*
- *Avatar*
- *Gettysburg*
- *Glory*
- *Miracle*

✦ Potential Courses That Relate to This Capacity

- *Anthropology courses*—cultural anthropology, social anthropology
- *Business courses*—organizational behavior, leadership or management skills
- *Communication courses*—interpersonal communication, small group communications
- *Leadership courses*
- *Political science courses*—political theory, political behavior

- *Psychology courses*—small group dynamics, social psychology, organizational psychology, human development, identity development
- *Sociology courses*—organizations, social institutions

✦ Notable Quotes

Coming together is a beginning. Keeping together is progress. Working together is success.—Henry Ford, inventor

Synergy is the highest activity of life; it creates new untapped alternatives; it values and exploits the mental, emotional, and psychological differences between people.—Stephen R. Covey, author, *The Seven Habits of Highly Effective People*

The key elements in the art of working together are how to deal with change, how to deal with conflict, and how to reach our potential . . . the needs of the team are best met when we meet the needs of individual persons.—Max DePree, author, *Leadership Jazz*

Organizational cultures are created by leaders, and one of the most decisive functions of leadership may well be the creation, the management, and—if and when that may become necessary—the destruction of culture.—Edgar Schein, author, *Organizational Culture and Leadership*

Culture is an integrated system of learned behavior patterns that are characteristic of the members of any given society. Culture

refers to the total way of life for a particular group of people. It includes [what] a group of people thinks, says, does and makes—its customs, language, material artifacts and shared systems of attitudes and feelings.—L. Robert Kohls, author

✦ Reflection Questions

- How well do you observe group dynamics in real time? What do you tend to pay the most attention to? What is hardest for you to learn?
- When was the last time you were blindsided by group dynamics? What were the circumstances? What was the result?
- What resources do you use to ensure that you have a good sense for the feelings, perceptions, and values of a group?
- How do leaders create an environment in which group dynamics are open and understood versus closed and underground?
- Think about an organization or group to which you belong. How would you describe the difference between the written and unwritten rules of the group?

Emotional Self-Perception

✦ Emotional Self-Perception Defined

In the *American Heritage Dictionary*, *self-perception* is defined as an awareness of the characteristics that constitute one's self; self-knowledge.

In essence, emotional self-perception is about identifying your emotions and reactions and their impact on you. Emotional self-perception means that individuals are acutely aware of their feelings (in real time). In addition, emotional self-perception means understanding how these feelings lead to behaviors. Having emotional self-perception also means that emotionally intelligent leaders have a choice as to how they respond. This capacity enables one to differentiate between the emotions felt and the actions taken. In most situations, both healthy and unhealthy responses are available.

✦ Too Much Emotional Self-Perception

Individuals who are too focused on emotional self-perception may lose themselves in their own self-analysis. They spend so much time thinking about themselves or trying to figure out what they think others want to see that they lose perspective or balance. When we spend too much energy on emotional self-perception, others may wonder who we really are or whether we understand the world around us. In addition, when we're too focused on emotional self-perception, we may spend a lot of energy on impression management and have a difficult time letting others in or self-disclosing. This may be challenging for those "others," because relationships are built on trust, and people need to trust that they are hearing from the real person, not an inauthentic person. In other words, at an extreme, too much emotional self-perception builds a wall that makes it difficult for others to create meaningful and authentic relationships with us.

← Too Little Emotional Self-Perception

Individuals who struggle with this capacity often find themselves captive to their emotions or, at the least, surprised by their emotional reactions. In essence, they may react immediately or instinctively to situations or a specific stimulus because of a lack of emotional self-perception. Because emotions lead to behavior, without emotional self-perception we may be more likely to demonstrate inappropriate, unproductive, or simply unhelpful behaviors. At an extreme, too little emotional self-perception makes us unaware of how our emotions are affecting others—and even how it affects ourselves. With low emotional self-perception, we may be oblivious to what is happening, which may erode trust with others and cause them to seek out a more stable leader.

← Student Quotes

Carefully watch and monitor the reactions of others when you display emotion. Try to gauge the strength and severity (either positive or negative reaction) to change your levels of emotional expression to best fit the group. If you feel the impact of your expression was regarded with more importance or impact than it should have been, you should not be afraid to explain or reiterate the true intention or meaning.

The best way I can demonstrate emotional self-perception is by never "taking things personally." By understanding that other team members are working from their own biases (but not trying to personally hurt me), I can identify that the actions of team members might affect me emotionally when they don't mean to. By understanding my emotional reaction to actions that other people take, I can avoid escalating any problem.

Someone demonstrates emotional self-perception by either choosing to act or not to act in a given situation. Often when [one is] a leader one has to choose not to outwardly act, regardless of what they are feeling inside. When a resident, for example, has noticed that what they are saying is not having an impact, often they will stop speaking or speak more loudly. If they notice that I am reacting adversely to what they are saying, often they will try to speak more loudly. I think good leaders take a step back and examine what they are doing and how it is affecting them. It's important to evaluate your actions to see if they are having a beneficial impact.

I think as a leader it is OK to identify your emotions and reactions. It is necessary to gain the trust of the people.

✦ Online Articles and Resources

- http://www.eiconsortium.org—Consortium for Research on Emotional Intelligence in Organizations
- http://www.unh.edu/emotional_intelligence—Emotional Intelligence Information
- http://www.eq.org—An internet directory on emotional intelligence
- http://www.reuvenbaron.org—The personal website of scholar Reuven Bar-On
- http://www.6seconds.org—Six Seconds

✦ Suggested Books

- *Becoming a Resonant Leader: Develop Your Emotional Intelligence, Renew Your Relationships, Sustain Your Effectiveness* by Richard E. Boyatzis, Fran Johnston, and Annie McKee
- *The Practicing Mind: Bringing Discipline and Focus into Your Life* by Thomas Sterner
- *Thoughts & Feelings: Taking Control of Your Moods and Your Life* by Matthew McKay, Martha David, and Patrick Fanning
- *Primal Leadership: Learning to Lead with Emotional Intelligence* by Daniel Goleman, Richard E. Boyatzis, and Annie McKee
- *Raising Your Emotional Intelligence: A Practical Guide* by Jeanne S. Segal
- *Don't Let Your Emotions Run Your Life: How Dialectical Behavior Therapy Can Put You in Control* by Scott Spradlin

✦ Suggested Films

The following films highlight the capacity of emotional self-perception. Some characters may overuse this capacity; others may lack the ability to use it successfully.

- *Primary Colors*
- *Wall Street*
- *Spider-Man*
- *Milk*
- *On Golden Pond*
- *Ordinary People*
- *The Dark Knight*
- *Falling Down*
- *Sid and Nancy*
- *The Wizard of Oz*
- *Remember the Titans*
- *Lord of the Rings* trilogy
- *Finding Nemo*
- *A League of Their Own*
- *Gandhi*

← Potential Courses That Relate to This Capacity

- *Biology courses*—neuroscience
- *Business courses*—organizational behavior, leadership or management skills
- *Communication courses*—interpersonal communication, small group communications
- *Leadership courses*
- *Psychology courses*—small group dynamics, human development, identity development, neuropsychology, social psychology
- *Theater courses*—acting, improvisational acting

← Notable Quotes

A clear understanding of negative emotions dismisses them.—Vernon Howard, author

Analysis gave me great freedom of emotions and fantastic confidence. I felt I had served my time as a puppet.—Hedy Lamarr, actress

Emotions get in the way but they don't pay me to start crying at the loss of 269 lives. They pay me to put some perspective on the situation.—Ted Koppel, journalist

Even before Watergate and his resignation, Nixon had inspired conflicting and passionate emotions.—Stephen Ambrose, historian and author

I choose not to give energy to the emotions of revenge, hatred, or the desire to subjugate.—Rosanne Cash, singer

I could work out a lot of my emotions by going to class and dancing.—Suzanne Farrell, ballerina

Reflection Questions

- Think about an individual who easily gets under your skin. What does this person do to push your buttons? What is your automatic response?

- What strategies can you put in place to diagnose and regulate your emotions in real time?
- In what ways does emotional self-perception benefit you as a leader?
- Who in your sphere of influence is an exemplary model of emotional self-perception?
- What emotions do you tend to feel in times of stress? In times of happiness? Be specific.

CAPACITY 4

Honest Self-Understanding

← Honest Self-Understanding Defined

In the *Stanford Encyclopedia of Philosophy*, *self-knowledge* is defined as knowledge of one's particular mental states, including one's beliefs, desires, and sensations.

Honest self-understanding is about being aware of your own strengths and limitations. Honest self-understanding means celebrating and honoring your strengths and talents while acknowledging and addressing your limitations. Honest self-understanding means accepting the good and bad about your personality, abilities, and ideas. When emotionally intelligent leaders demonstrate honest self-understanding, they embody a foundational capacity of effective leadership—the ability to see a more holistic self and understand how this impacts their leadership.

← Too Much Honest Self-Understanding

At one extreme, when we focus too much on honest self-understanding we may be lost in an endless quest to get to know our "self." A theme song could be "I Still Haven't Found What I'm Looking For" by U2. Too much time and energy spent on honest self-understanding leads to difficulty in creating and maintaining healthy relationships. In the context of leadership, this makes it difficult for us to gain traction with a group or organization. Also, others may perceive us as wishy-washy and noncommittal because we simply do not have a clear idea of which way to go (at an individual and organizational level). This lack of direction comes from too much focus on self. At another extreme, when we focus too much on honest self-understanding, this may lead others to see us as self-centered. If we are hyper-aware of what we do well and don't do well, and we spend time publicly talking about all of it, others may perceive us as conceited, selfish, or so focused inwardly that others do not matter to us.

← Too Little Honest Self-Understanding

Individuals with low levels of honest self-understanding will likely frustrate others with their lack of self-awareness. These individuals often lack a sense of what they do well or don't do well. This may lead to a lack of follow-through, ineffectiveness, or major problems with accomplishing tasks. Some who lack honest self-understanding are perceived as not caring about what others think or feel. They may say things like, "I am me, and since this is who I am, if they don't like me, so what?" When put into a leadership role, these people often alienate others or have a hard time developing a sense of team among members of the group. Others who demonstrate low levels of honest self-understanding care how they are perceived, but lack the skills and/or initiative to improve themselves. Regardless of the details, low levels of honest self-understanding generally yield frustration and exhaustion for those with whom this person works.

← **Student Quotes**

It is crucial to know your strengths, feelings, etc. By knowing and being in touch with these you can more effectively control them and put them to use.

Leaders guide the organization and thus are looked to [to] provide an environment that is conducive to the organization's success. Leaders who are not stable or who cannot reasonably control their emotions place the entire group as well as the individual members in a state of flux that is most likely neither healthy nor conducive to progress.

When a leader understands herself, she can identify her biases and try to eliminate them from interactions with teammates. For example, I know that punctuality is personally important to me, but that some people are habitually late. I can deal with the problem of tardiness without an emotional reaction if I remember my own biases.

Ideally a leader is aware of his or her own strengths and weaknesses. This self-understanding can then be shared with the group they are trying to lead so that they understand how the leader operates. Possibly more important though, an individual's self-understanding encourages others to pursue an understanding of themselves as well.

A leader's self-understanding or lack thereof can affect others in many ways. If a leader does not understand and accept himself fully, he will not help others to the extent he should be able to. On the other hand, when a leader accepts himself and understands himself, he is capable of helping others do so as well.

✦ Online Articles and Resources

- http://www.inc.com—Self-Awareness and the Effective Leader
- http://www.leadershipnow.com—Emotional Intelligence: Self-Awareness
- http://books.google.com—An Essay Concerning Human Understanding by John Locke
- http://www.eiconsortium.org—Consortium for Research on Emotional Intelligence in Organizations
- http://www.unh.edu/emotional_intelligence—Emotional Intelligence Information
- http://www.eq.org—An Internet directory on emotional intelligence
- http://www.reuvenbaron.org—The personal website of scholar Reuven Bar-On
- http://www.6seconds.org—Six Seconds

✦ Suggested Books

- *The Artist's Way Workbook* by Julia Cameron
- *Learning to Lead: A Workbook on Becoming a Leader* by Warren Bennis
- *The Leadership Challenge Workbook* by James M. Kouzes and Barry Z. Posner

- *Waking Up to Resonance and Renewal: Charting a Path to Self-Awareness and Great Leadership* by Richard E. Boyatzis and Annie McKee
- *Beyond Effective: Practices in Self-Aware Leadership* by David Peck
- *Principle-Centered Leadership* by Stephen R. Covey
- *What Type Am I? The Myers-Briggs Type Indicator Made Easy* by Renee Baron
- *Journal to the Self: Twenty-Two Paths to Personal Growth—Open the Door to Self-Understanding by Writing, Reading, and Creating a Journal of Your Life* by Kathleen Adams
- *Personality Plus: How to Understand Others by Understanding Yourself* by Florence Littauer
- *The Enneagram Made Easy: Discover the 9 Types of People* by Renee Baron and Elizabeth Wagele

✦ Suggested Television Shows

The following television shows highlight the capacity of honest self-understanding. Some characters may overuse this capacity; others may lack the ability to use it successfully.

- *30 Rock*
- *The Office*
- *Lost*
- *Modern Family*
- *The Fashion Show/Project Runway*
- *Top Chef*
- *The Real World*
- *The Oprah Winfrey Show*
- *Seinfeld*

✦ Potential Courses That Relate to This Capacity

- *Business courses*—organizational behavior, leadership or management skills
- *Communication courses*—interpersonal communication, small group communications
- *Leadership courses*
- *Psychology courses*—social psychology, identity development
- *Theater courses*—acting, improvisational acting

✦ Notable Quotes

O, happy the soul that saw its own faults.—Rumi, poet and philosopher

People of the world don't look at themselves, and so they blame one another.—Rumi, poet and philosopher

Everything that irritates us about others can lead us to an understanding of ourselves.—Carl Jung, psychologist

Everyone thinks of changing the world, but no one thinks of changing himself.—Leo Tolstoy, author, *War and Peace*

Know thyself.—Socrates, philosopher

To have greater self awareness or understanding means to have a better grasp of reality. —The Dalai Lama, spiritual leader

← Reflection Questions

- What role does feedback play in honest self-understanding? Is the thought of asking others for feedback worrisome to you? If not, what is holding you back from doing so?
- When you are in the midst of struggling with a weakness of yours, can you recognize it happening in real time? What happens?
- Do you give yourself credit for strengths you bring to the table? What environment would best use your strengths?
- Who in your sphere of influence will provide you with honest feedback? Do you seek it out on a regular basis?

CAPACITY 5

Healthy Self-Esteem

✦ Healthy Self-Esteem Defined

In the *American Heritage Dictionary*, *self-esteem* is defined as pride in oneself; self-respect.

Healthy self-esteem is about having a balanced sense of self. Emotionally intelligent leaders possess a high level of self-worth, are confident in their abilities, and are willing to stand up for what they believe in. They are also balanced by a sense of humility and the ability to create space for the opinions, perspectives, and thoughts of others.

✦ Too Much Healthy Self-Esteem

Individuals with too much self-esteem may come across as arrogant, ignorant, or lacking concern for others. When self-esteem is taken to an extreme, others may perceive us as concerned only with self. In a leadership context, this creates a challenge for us, because positive leadership, at its core, is about trusting relationships between people. Too much self-esteem also causes us to overestimate ourselves and our abilities, which often leads us to overcommit or overconfidence. In addition, with an excessive level of confidence we may exclude others from being involved.

← Too Little Healthy Self-Esteem

Those who lack self-esteem suffer from a lack of confidence or belief in their abilities or ideas. Displaying too little self-esteem may make us appear to be uncomfortable making decisions or speaking in front of a group. At an extreme, we may overcompensate for too little self-esteem by acting confident without really believing it, which can make us rigid or cause us to lash out when challenged by others. This diminishes trust and decreases the likelihood that others will get involved or want to contribute.

← Student Quotes

Healthy self-esteem is being comfortable with who you are. People say that it doesn't matter what other people think, but I don't think this is true; I think good self-esteem is being OK with what others think about you. Self-esteem is hard to define, but you know it when you see someone who is confident.

Healthy self-esteem is not arrogance, but an ability to interact with others in a positive and rational manner that exudes some form of personal acceptance of being comfortable with one's self.

Healthy self-esteem can be seen across a room. First, the person has good posture and a pleasant manner. When I talk to the person, she replies without qualifications and with no apologies for her opinions. But the person is not arrogant. She carefully considers her thoughts and is willing to change her opinions when good evidence is presented. Her self-worth is not tied to being correct all the time.

Healthy self-esteem is like a tree. A fully grown tree stands tall and strong and sure of itself. The most important part is even though the tree is large, tall, and strong with broad leaves and thick branches, there is still always room for growth.

✦ Online Articles and Resources

- http://www.fsu.edu/profiles/baumeister—Roy Baumeister, scholar
- http://viewonbuddhism.org—A View on Buddhism
- http://www.jrf.org.uk—Self-esteem: The costs and causes of low self-worth
- http://www.nytimes.com—The Trouble with Self-Esteem
- http://www.papillonsartpalace.com—Exploding the Self-Esteem Myth

✦ Suggested Books

- *Self-Esteem: A Proven Program of Cognitive Techniques for Assessing, Improving, and Maintaining Your Self-Esteem* by Matthew McKay and Patrick Fanning
- *The Self-Esteem Workbook* by Glenn R. Schiraldi

- *The Self-Esteem Companion: Simple Exercises to Help You Challenge Your Inner Critic & Celebrate Your Personal Strengths* by Patrick Fanning, Carole Honeychurch, Catharine Sutker, and Matthew McKay
- *Breaking the Chain of Low Self-Esteem* by Marilyn Sorensen
- *The Cultural Animal: Human Nature, Meaning, and Social Life* by Roy F. Baumeister
- *Attitudes, Beliefs and Choices* by Alexandra Delis-Abrams
- *The Confidence Plan: How to Build a Stronger You* by Tim Ursiny

✦ Suggested Films

The following films highlight the capacity of healthy self-esteem. Some characters may overuse this capacity; others may lack the ability to use it successfully.

- *Billy Elliot*
- *The Full Monty*
- *Ratatouille*
- *Dead Poets Society*
- *Kung Fu Panda*
- *Erin Brockovich*
- *Powder*
- *Finding Nemo*
- *The Shawshank Redemption*
- *Good Will Hunting*
- *Apollo 13*
- *Courage Under Fire*
- *Jonathan Livingston Seagull*
- *Norma Rae*
- *The Wizard of Oz*

✦ Potential Courses That Relate to This Capacity

- *Leadership courses*
- *Philosophy courses*
- *Psychology courses*—small group dynamics, industrial and organizational psychology, social psychology, personality theory, human development
- *Theater courses*—acting

✦ Notable Quotes

You yourself, as much as anybody in the entire universe, deserve your love and affection.—Siddhartha Gautama, founder of Buddhism

Never be bullied into silence. Never allow yourself to be made a victim. Accept no one's definition of your life; define yourself. —Harvey Fierstein, actor and playwright

Every individual has a place to fill in the world, and is important, in some respect, whether he chooses to be so or not.—Nathaniel Hawthorne, author

Self confidence is the first requisite to great undertakings. —Dr. Samuel Johnson, author

If only you could sense how important you are to the lives of those you meet; how important you can be to people you may never even dream of. There is something of yourself that you leave at every meeting with another person.—Fred Rogers, host of *Mr. Rogers' Neighborhood*

You can do what you have to do, and sometimes you can do it even better than you think you can.—Jimmy Carter, thirty-ninth president of the United States of America

If you want a quality, act as if you already had it.—William James, psychologist and philosopher

Never bend your head. Always hold it high. Look the world straight in the face.—Helen Keller, author

← Reflection Questions

- In what environments is your self-esteem challenged the most?
- Who makes you feel good about your ideas, thoughts, dreams, and aspirations?
- What happens when a leader lacks healthy self-esteem? How does this affect others?
- Who in your network of friendships exemplifies healthy self-esteem for you? What is it about this person that stands out for you?

Emotional Self-Control

✦ Emotional Self-Control Defined

In the *American Heritage Dictionary*, *self-control* is defined as control of one's emotions, desires, or actions by one's own will.

Emotional self-control is about consciously moderating your emotions and reactions. Although feeling emotions and being aware of them is part of this, so too is regulating them. Emotional self-control is about both awareness (being conscious of feelings) and action (managing emotions and knowing when and how to show them). Recognizing feelings, understanding how and when to demonstrate those feelings appropriately, and taking responsibility for your emotions (versus being a victim of them) are critical components of this capacity.

✦ Too Much Emotional Self-Control

Those who are too focused on keeping their emotions in check may struggle when working to motivate and engage others. Like everyone else, leaders feel joy, frustration, excitement, anger, and the like. If harnessed constructively, these emotions can translate to action, but too much control may cause us to hide all our emotions. Additionally, when we are too focused on emotional self-control we may misunderstand the power of our own emotions. Missing opportunities to express emotions can be painful or unfortunate experiences, for those stifling their emotions and for those around them. Stifling emotions, or holding emotions back, doesn't necessarily lead to better results. Rarely do people want to interact with someone who seems robotic, which is how people can perceive someone who is too focused on emotional self-control. Imagine if Rosa Parks had stifled her emotions!

← Too Little Emotional Self-Control

Those of us who struggle to keep our emotions under control are likely to encounter many hardships along the way. First, we may be unaware of how our emotions are affecting those who follow. If our emotions are consistently negative, we are likely to find ourselves alone, or with few others around. And although people may be capable of following someone who exudes negative emotions frequently or without abandon, they may be following out of fear or frustration. At the other extreme, those who are too positive may also experience challenges, such as realizing that those who interact with them feel overwhelmed, frustrated, or apathetic. In general, those who struggle with this capacity may undermine their ability to build trust and confidence in others. People need some level of consistency in relationships with others, and individuals with too little emotional self-control often struggle with regulating their emotions. This behavior may make others feel like they're "walking on eggshells" around such a leader, which is not conducive to healthy relationships or building a team.

← **Student Quotes**

I was working under a person who would continuously use my ideas. He would also pawn off mistakes that he had made on us. On many occasions I wanted to give him a piece of my mind using as many profanities as possible, but we were being watched by others at all times, whether we knew it or not, and had to act accordingly. It was hard, because I am only human and I am young. I am still driven by my emotions and I need to develop strategies to control them.

As a student leader dealing with disciplinary actions, I have frequently had to moderate my emotions. Removing my emotion helped me see beyond a solitary event and see how solving the underlying problem might improve that individual's life in the long term.

[Emotional control] happens daily. When a member of an organization screws up, does something stupid, or simply does not do what was expected, it is extremely frustrating. Rather than channel my internal negative energy outward, I understand what it is that I am feeling and verbalize it to my members. The ability to understand and verbalize emotions is an essential element to personal understanding and communication.

I've had to moderate my emotions when in front of other members of an organization who were not paying attention and not following directions. I had to keep myself calm to describe what they were doing wrong to help them do things correctly. It can be difficult because we are often under time constraints.

✦ Online Articles and Resources

- http://www.helium.com—Emotional Self-Control: Steps to Overcoming Reactive Patterns
- http://news.softpedia.com—How to Get Emotional Self-Control: Simply Speak Your Mind, Scientists Say
- http://www.eiconsortium.org—Consortium for Research on Emotional Intelligence in Organizations
- http://www.unh.edu/emotional_intelligence—Emotional Intelligence Information
- http://www.eq.org—An Internet directory on emotional intelligence
- http://www.reuvenbaron.org—The personal website of scholar Reuven Bar-On
- http://www.6seconds.org—Six Seconds

✦ Suggested Books

- *Emotional Discipline: The Power to Choose How You Feel; 5 Life Changing Steps to Feeling Better Every Day* by Charles Manz
- *Becoming a Resonant Leader: Develop Your Emotional Intelligence, Renew Your Relationships, Sustain Your Effectiveness* by Richard E. Boyatzis, Fran Johnston, and Annie McKee

- *Emotional Intelligence: Why It Can Matter More Than IQ* (10th anniversary edition) by Daniel Goleman
- *Working with Emotional Intelligence* by Daniel Goleman
- *Building Emotional Intelligence: Techniques to Cultivate Inner Strength in Children* by Linda Lantieri and Daniel Goleman
- *Primal Leadership: Learning to Lead with Emotional Intelligence* by Daniel Goleman, Richard E. Boyatzis, and Annie McKee
- *Raising Your Emotional Intelligence: A Practical Guide* by Jeanne S. Segal

❖ Suggested Films

The following films highlight the capacity of emotional self-control. Some characters may overuse this capacity; others may lack the ability to use it successfully.

- *Transformers*
- *The Chronicles of Narnia*
- *Hancock*
- *Ordinary People*
- *Spider-Man*
- *Avatar*
- *Step Brothers*
- *Ice Age*
- *The Wizard of Oz*
- *Shrek*
- *As Good as It Gets*
- *The Odd Couple*
- *Harold and Maude*
- *Billy Madison*
- *Finding Nemo*

← Potential Courses That Relate to This Capacity

- *Business courses*—organizational behavior, leadership or management skills
- *Communication courses*—small group communications
- *Leadership courses*
- *Psychology courses*—small group dynamics, industrial and organizational psychology, social psychology, introductory psychology

← Notable Quotes

Let's not forget that the little emotions are the great captains of our lives and we obey them without realizing it.—Vincent Van Gogh, artist

Any emotion, if it is sincere, is involuntary.—Mark Twain, author

When dealing with people, remember you are not dealing with creatures of logic, but creatures of emotion.—Dale Carnegie, author of *How to Win Friends and Influence People*

The emotions aren't always immediately subject to reason, but they are always immediately subject to action.—William James, psychologist and philosopher

He liked to observe emotions; they were like red lanterns strung along the dark unknown of another's personality, marking vulnerable points.—Ayn Rand, author

People don't ask for facts in making up their minds. They would rather have one good, soul-satisfying emotion than a dozen facts.—Robert Keith Leavitt, author

Reflection Questions

- When leading others, what are your "hot buttons"? What actions of others tend to challenge, frustrate, and anger you?
- What techniques do you use (in real time) to regulate your emotions?
- Who do you know who best models emotional self-control?
- Think of a time when you were with someone who demonstrated a lack of emotional self-control. How did you feel as an observer of the situation? What was the impact on others?
- When did you last fail to regulate your emotions when leading others? How did this affect the group? How did it affect your credibility?

CAPACITY 7

Authenticity

✦ Authenticity Defined

In the *American Heritage Dictionary*, *authenticity* is defined as the quality or condition of being authentic, trustworthy, or genuine.

Authenticity is a complex concept that emphasizes the importance of being trustworthy and transparent and living in a way in which your words match your actions and vice versa. This is no small order. Emotionally intelligent leaders who are authentic follow through on commitments and present themselves and their motives in an open and honest manner.

✦ Too Much Authenticity

Those who are too focused on authenticity may be overly concerned with the thoughts and perceptions of others. Ironically, consumed as they are with the perceptions of others, they may lose sight of their authentic self. Too much emphasis on authenticity may lead to an appearance of arrogance and self-righteousness. Another attribute of those demonstrating too much authenticity is a lack of progress and results with others. Because relationships are a focal point, tasks and activities focused on accomplishing goals may become secondary, and the group may stall and fail to be productive.

✦ Too Little Authenticity

Those who lack authenticity will have a difficult time gaining the trust of others. Because authenticity means that others perceive them to be trustworthy, lacking authenticity complicates their efforts to be effective leaders. Leadership is an activity grounded in trust. If a relationship lacks trust, others will have a difficult time following, and these leaders will find themselves in a challenging position. To a lesser extent, those who lack authenticity may be seen as "all talk and no action," especially if they do not follow through on commitments. In the end, people who lack this capacity often resort to using formal power to remain in control. The hearts of others will no longer be fully invested in the relationship or task, and these leaders will be left with a group that, at best, complies with directions set forth, but with little motivation or investment in the effort.

✦ Student Quotes

An authentic leader is humble, intelligent, analytical, is accepting of responsibility and consequences, and would not ask a follower to do anything that he himself would not do.

An authentic leader does not try to take credit for the work of the entire group. An authentic leader will have sincere concerns for the well-being of his group members and the outcome of the group's work.

An authentic leader is someone who is consistent in their actions. An authentic leader would be the same person on the inside that they are projecting on the outside.

An authentic leader will have sincere concerns for the well-being of his group members and the outcome of the group's work.

✦ Online Articles and Resources

- http://personalpages.manchester.ac.uk—The Authentic Personality
- http://psych.athabascau.ca—Authentic Life
- http://www.hbs.edu/mba/academics/coursecatalog/2090.html—Authentic Leadership Development
- http://youtube.com—Bill George—A Unique Life Story
- http://www.mindgarden.com—The Authentic Leadership Questionnaire

✦ Suggested Books

- *Selfhood and Authenticity* by Corey Anton
- *Authentic Leadership: Rediscovering the Secrets to Creating Lasting Value* by Bill George
- *True North: Discover Your Authentic Leadership* by Bill George, David Gergen, and Peter Sims
- *Finding Your True North: A Personal Guide* by Bill George, Andrew McLean, and Nick Craig

- *Authentic Leadership: Courage in Action* by Robert W. Terry
- *Building an Authentic Leadership Image* by Center for Creative Leadership, Corey Criswell, and David P. Campbell
- *Leadership from the Inside Out: Becoming a Leader for Life* by Kevin Cashman
- *High Impact Leader: Moments Matter in Authentic Leadership Development* by Bruce Avolio and Fred Luthans
- *Jonathan Livingston Seagull* by Richard Bach

✦ Suggested Films

The following films highlight the capacity of authenticity. Some characters may overuse this capacity; others may lack the ability to use it successfully.

- *Empire of the Sun*
- *Whale Rider*
- *Rain Man*
- *Dead Poets Society*
- *Pushing Hands*
- *Billy Elliot*
- *Finding Forrester*
- *Good Will Hunting*
- *Toy Story*
- *The Devil Wears Prada*
- *True Colors*

✦ Potential Courses That Relate to This Capacity

- *Business courses*—organizational behavior, leadership or management skills
- *Communication courses*—interpersonal communication, small group communications, organizational communications
- *Leadership courses*

- *Philosophy courses*—ethics, social philosophy
- *Psychology courses*—small group dynamics, social psychology, personality theory, human development

← Notable Quotes

Honesty and transparency make you vulnerable. Be honest and transparent anyway.—Mother Theresa, founder of Missionaries of Charity

If you tell the truth, you don't have to remember anything.—Mark Twain, author

To find yourself, think for yourself.—Socrates, philosopher

Let the people know the truth and the country is safe.—Abraham Lincoln, sixteenth president of the United States of America

There is but one cause of failure and that is a man's lack of faith in his true self.—William James, psychologist and philosopher

The truth is the kindest thing we can give folks in the end.—Harriet Beecher Stowe, author, *Uncle Tom's Cabin*

◆ Reflection Questions

- As you reflect on the definition of authenticity, what does it mean to you? How do you display authenticity when working with others?
- In what areas of life do you have a difficult time bringing your authentic self to the table? Why is this the case?
- In what ways might someone be seen as inauthentic? How does that impact his or her ability to lead others?
- In what cases might it be appropriate to act in an inauthentic manner?

CAPACITY 8

Flexibility

✦ Flexibility Defined

In the *American Heritage Dictionary*, *flexibility* is defined as susceptible to influence or persuasion; tractable.

Flexibility is about being open and adaptive to changing situations. The best-laid plans don't always come to fruition, so emotionally intelligent leaders need to be responsive to change and open to feedback. By thinking creatively and using their problem-solving skills, emotionally intelligent leaders engage others in determining a new way to reach their goals.

✦ Too Much Flexibility

A person who displays too much flexibility may be viewed as "wishy-washy" and unable to make a concrete decision. In addition, too much flexibility can often be a way to avoid confrontation—but this allows issues and challenges to fester without resolution. Another challenge for individuals who are too flexible may be that others perceive them as lacking principles, focus, or direction. For example, if they make a decision and then spend significant time entertaining other options and changing their minds throughout the process, progress stalls. Too much flexibility may lead someone to become lost in the possibilities.

← Too Little Flexibility

Individuals who lack flexibility will have a difficult time working with a diverse group of people. Stuck in their own way of being or leading, inflexible people can become rigid in their approach and have trouble creating space for others to feel a part of the dialogue or action. And at some point, others in the group may take a stand against the current course of action or decision. When this happens, if the person lacks flexibility, discord and conflict are likely to emerge among group members. When someone lacks flexibility, others get the message (intended or otherwise) that this person does not care, does not listen, and does not value the input of others.

← Student Quotes

Flexibility allows a leader to experiment with all the opinions and ideas shared within the group, which enables them to find the best path for their goals. Experimenting too much can waste time and make the leader appear insecure in their decisions.

Flexibility is an asset for a leader. It allows them to appear more accommodating to others. However, too much flexibility can lead to disorganization.

Flexibility can be good or bad. While it is good to try new things, being too flexible could result in disaster.

Flexibility equals versatility in many cases, and allows a leader to move with ease from one situation to another. However, if a leader is too flexible, it may lead to subordinates taking advantage of the leader.

Online Articles and Resources

- http://ezinearticles.com—Foundations of Leadership III—Flexibility and Adaptability
- http://www.fastcompany.com/blog—Leadership & Flexibility: What We Can Learn From "The Elevator"
- http://www.youtube.com—Super Flexibility in Leadership
- http://www.versatileleader.com—The Versatile Leader
- http://www.kenblanchard.com—The Ken Blanchard Companies

Suggested Books

- *The Versatile Leader* by Bob Kaplan and Rob Kaiser
- *Leading at a Higher Level: Blanchard on Leadership and Creating High Performing Organizations* by Ken Blanchard
- *Leadership and the One Minute Manager: Increasing Effectiveness Through Situational Leadership* by Ken Blanchard, Patricia Zigarmi, and Drea Zigarmi
- *Our Iceberg Is Melting: Changing and Succeeding Under Any Conditions* by John Kotter and Holger Rathgeber

- *Primal Leadership: Learning to Lead with Emotional Intelligence* by Daniel Goleman, Richard E. Boyatzis, and Annie McKee
- *Who Moved My Cheese?* by Spencer Johnson

✦ Suggested Films

The following films highlight the capacity of flexibility. Some characters may overuse this capacity; others may lack the ability to use it successfully.

- *The Candidate*
- *The Hunt for Red October*
- *Harry Potter* series
- *A Few Good Men*
- *Hancock*
- *Spider-Man*
- *The Last King of Scotland*
- *Pirates of the Caribbean* series
- *The Queen*
- *Thirteen Days*
- *Apollo 13*
- *Shrek*
- *Miss Congeniality*
- *The Devil Wears Prada*

✦ Potential Courses That Relate to This Capacity

- *Business courses*—organizational behavior, leadership or management skills
- *Communication courses*—interpersonal communication, persuasive communication theory, small group communications, organizational communications

- *Leadership courses*
- *Political science courses*—comparative politics, international relations
- *Psychology courses*—small group dynamics, industrial and organizational psychology, social psychology
- *Theater courses*—acting, improvisational acting

✦ Notable Quotes

Whatever is flexible and flowing will tend to grow, whatever is rigid and blocked will wither and die.—*Tao Te Ching*

Empty your mind, be formless, shapeless—like water. Now you put water into a cup, it becomes the cup, you put water into a bottle, it becomes the bottle, you put it in a teapot, it becomes the teapot. Now water can flow or it can crash. Be water, my friend.—Bruce Lee, actor

Flexibility—in all aspects of life, the person with the most varied responses "wins."—Kelly Perdew, author, *Take Command: 10 Leadership Principles I Learned in the Military*

As any jazz musician knows, it takes flexibility and adaptability for improvisation to create beauty.—Doc Childre and Bruce Cryer, authors, *From Chaos to Coherence*

New ideas stir from every corner. They show up disguised inno-cently as interruptions, contradictions, and embarrassing dilem-mas. Beware of total strangers and friends alike who shower you with comfortable sameness, and remain open to those who make you uneasy, for they are the true messengers of the future.—Rob Lebow, author, *A Journey into the Heroic Environment*

God turns you from one feeling to another and teaches by means of opposites, so that you will have two wings to fly, not one.—Rumi, poet and philosopher

✦ Reflection Questions

- What is the right balance of flexibility and rigidity for you as a leader? What does it look like? Describe a time when you had this experience.
- Do you need high levels of self-awareness to effectively demonstrate the capacity of flexibility? Why or why not?
- Can you think of a time when you were too flexible in leading a group? What happened as a result?
- What does the quote from the *Tao Te Ching* in the Notable Quotes section mean to you?
- Who do you think of when you imagine leaders who are flexible and effective in their role? What do you imagine are their challenges?

CAPACITY 9

Achievement

✦ Achievement Defined

In the *American Heritage Dictionary*, *achievement* is defined as something accomplished successfully, especially by means of exertion, skill, practice, or perseverance.

Achievement is about being driven to improve according to personal standards. Individuals often know achievement when they see and feel it. Instead of letting others define what achievement looks like, emotionally intelligent leaders pursue their passions and goals to a self-determined level of accomplishment. This drive produces results and may inspire others to become more focused in their efforts or at increased levels as well.

People are often motivated to achieve a goal because someone important to them (such as a parent, friend, or boss) sees it as important. Consider, instead, what you care deeply about—what do you have a passion for? A musical instrument? A hobby or an artistic medium? A sport? An issue or cause? No matter what our passion is, this drive produces results through a process infused with energy and desire.

✦ Too Much Achievement

At one extreme, those who are too focused on achievement may forget the human and relationship dynamics of being in an organization or group with others. Many individuals with high levels of achievement can produce so prodigiously that others around them may be left behind and feel like they have no role. In addition, those with a high level of achievement may become frustrated with others and their inability to do the work at the expected or desired level of performance. This feeling may lead to an attitude of "I will just do this myself"—which turns people off and ultimately creates the perception that the leader is a demanding taskmaster. When we are too focused on achievement, we can easily alienate ourselves from others—and find ourselves alone in a crowd.

✦ Too Little Achievement

Individuals with low levels of achievement will frustrate others when working on projects or tasks, especially if others are depending on them to accomplish a task. When someone fails to achieve, it presents a challenge to teamwork, group work at any level, and even social relationships. Low levels of achievement often manifest in several different forms. A common example is when there is inconsistency between what we say we will do and what we actually get done. We may miss meetings, fail to meet obligations, or lack follow-through. We may say "Yes, no problem" to a request but have difficulty actually following through with the commitment—the classic "overpromise and underdeliver" scenario. Or we may respond only when a request is placed in our lap—in other words, we take no initiative to go above and beyond what's expected. In its most extreme form, low achievement leads to a total abdication of responsibility, so we do nothing.

← Student Quotes

Students with a healthy level of achievement have experienced leadership, have studied their field extensively, and have broadened their understandings. However, I don't think that students should be busy every moment of the day. I think that reflection and friendly interaction with other students are important.

As long as a student goes out, gets involved, and attempts to make a difference while balancing school work, health, and a social life, I think the attributes of achievement are healthy.

Achievement is relative. Too often we fall into this paradigm that achievement is measured by grades and resume. My view staunchly differs . . . I think that every student is different. I do believe that one should not only excel academically but should excel in their personal life as well. Get involved in something that interests you. Take roles that are to your capability level and push those roles to their max. I don't think that everyone should be involved in five things but a balance between the two should be achieved.

A person is achieving at a satisfactory level when, at the end of
each day, they can sit down and ask themselves the question:
Was I productive today? Am I satisfied with what I did today? If
a person is satisfied with their achievements each and every day,
this is a healthy level.

✦ Online Articles and Resources

- http://www.youtube.com—Dr. Wayne Dyer—The Power of
  Intention
- http://www.mindtools.com—Personal Goal Setting
- http://www.mindtools.com—Locke's Goal Setting Theory—
  Understanding SMART Goal Setting
- http://www.12manage.com—Theory of Needs

✦ Suggested Books

- *Flow: The Psychology of Optimal Experience* by Mihaly
  Csikszentmihalyi
- *Finding Flow: The Psychology of Engagement with Everyday
  Life* by Mihaly Csikszentmihalyi
- *It's Not About the Bike* by Lance Armstrong
- *NLP: The New Technology of Achievement* by NLP
  Comprehensive, Steve Andreas, and Charles Faulkner
- *How They Achieved: Stories of Personal Achievement and
  Business Success* by Lucinda Watson
- *Art of Achievement: Mastering the 7 C's of Success in Business
  and Life* by Tom Morris
- *Finding Your Zone: Ten Core Lessons for Achieving Peak
  Performance in Sports and Life* by Michael Lardon and David
  Leadbetter

- *The Power of Intention* by Wayne Dyer
- *The Magic of Thinking Big* by David Schwartz

❧ Suggested Films

The following films highlight the capacity of achievement. Some characters may overuse this capacity; others may lack the ability to use it successfully.

- *Spellbound*
- *Up*
- *Searching for Bobby Fischer*
- *The Karate Kid*
- *Bend It Like Beckham*
- *Avatar*
- *Slumdog Millionaire*
- *Mad Hot Ballroom*
- *Star Trek* (2009)
- *Kung Fu Panda*
- *Miracle*
- *Rudy*

❧ Potential Courses That Relate to This Capacity

- *Business courses*—organizational behavior, leadership or management skills, human resources
- *Career development courses*
- *Communication courses*—interpersonal communication, small group communications
- *Leadership courses*
- *Psychology courses*—small group dynamics, social psychology

← Notable Quotes

You have to learn the rules of the game. And then you have to play better than anyone else.—Albert Einstein, theoretical physicist

It is not the mountain we conquer but ourselves.—Sir Edmund Hillary, mountaineer

That some achieve great success, is proof to all that others can achieve it as well.—Abraham Lincoln, sixteenth president of the United States of America

If you have a task to perform and are vitally interested in it, excited and challenged by it, then you will exert maximum energy. But in the excitement, the pain of fatigue dissipates, and the exuberance of what you hope to achieve overcomes the weariness.—Jimmy Carter, thirty-ninth president of the United States of America

The three great essentials to achieve anything worthwhile are, first, hard work; second, stick-to-itiveness; third, common sense.—Thomas Edison, inventor

Satisfaction does not come with achievement, but with effort. Full effort is full victory.—Mohandas Gandhi, leader of the Indian Nationalist Movement

Leaders are made, they are not born. They are made by hard effort, which is the price which all of us must pay to achieve any goal that is worthwhile.—Vince Lombardi, football coach, Notre Dame University

✦ Reflection Questions

- How would you describe your level of achievement? On what basis do you make this claim?
- Would you say you are balanced in terms of achievement or at one extreme or the other? What are the consequences?
- When was the last time you had a laser-like focus on achieving something? What was it? What brought you into that zone? Could it be re-created?
- Achievement is often viewed as the accomplishment of tasks or goals. What are other, less tangible achievements that you accomplish every day?
- Think about an organization you're part of. What defines a high achiever? How do others react to the current benchmark?

CAPACITY 10

Optimism

✦ Optimism Defined

In the *American Heritage Dictionary*, *optimism* is defined as a tendency to expect the best possible outcome or dwell on the most hopeful aspects of a situation.

Emotionally intelligent leaders demonstrate a healthy, positive outlook and display a positive regard for the future. Optimism is a powerful force that many overlook. When demonstrated effectively, optimism is contagious and spreads throughout a group or organization.

Too often, optimism is assumed to be a trait that you either have or don't have. In fact, optimism is also a learned skill—the more often we see the positive, work to identify the best, and encourage others to be better, the more often we can produce those results. With optimism, we focus on the best possible outcome; as such, we align our thoughts in that way and work toward achieving that outcome.

⟵ Too Much Optimism

Interestingly, too much optimism can be a major flaw. After all, everyday life, whether personal or organizational, is not always rosy. With too much optimism, people tend to ignore or forget that conflict, disagreement, and challenges inevitably face them and others. Individuals demonstrating too much optimism likely have not been honest with themselves in facing difficulty, pain, or hardship; in fact, they could be denying reality. Too much optimism may blind us to limitations and areas of work that are essential for personal or organizational growth. If we ignore these areas, unresolved issues can persist and cause even greater problems. In essence, too much optimism can result in a failure to pursue problem solving, conflict resolution, and decision making; this neglect can lead to low morale and frustration among group members.

⟵ Too Little Optimism

Individuals with too little optimism can easily have a negative influence on those around them. For organizations, too little optimism can drag down organizational progress and morale. For individuals, too little optimism means pessimism, which affects personal health, relationships, and motivation. Leaders who lack optimism display it in a number of ways. First, they may simply shoot down the ideas of others and consistently find fault in their contributions. Individuals may also demonstrate low optimism when they consistently fail to acknowledge the accomplishments of others or the group. A lack of optimism manifests as a negative attitude that others find unpleasant to be around. A more subtle form of low optimism is a person's inability or ineffectual struggle to inspire others to accomplish a goal or achieve a better future.

✦ Student Quotes

If the leaders are pessimistic and never praise the work that has already been completed, employees' morale will dip and they will be unmotivated to maintain their current levels of production.

Individuals are unlikely to follow someone who is not excited about what they are doing. A sense of optimism and excitement may be the single thing that brings an individual to a meeting or to work; they look forward to being surrounded by a positive environment where success is pursued.

When the leader believes that a task cannot be done, it becomes impossible. But when the leader believes that it is possible, then world records are broken.

Optimism is a key ingredient to leadership. An optimistic leader has the ability to inspire followers, gain trust and support, and works to make a positive impact on people. Optimism is necessary for a successful endeavor.

✦ Online Articles and Resources

- http://www.newsweek.com/id/61572—This Is Your Brain on Optimism
- http://harvardmagazine.com—Muscle of Optimism
- http://leadershipchallenge.typepad.com—Inspire a Shared Vision

- http://hbr.harvardbusiness.org—To Lead, Create a Shared Vision
- http://www.apa.org—Seligman Touts the Art of Arguing with Yourself
- http://news.bbc.co.uk—The Happiness Formula
- http://www.authentichappiness.sas.upenn.edu/Default .aspx—University of Pennsylvania, Positive Psychology Center

✦ Suggested Books

- *Primal Leadership: Realizing the Power of Emotional Intelligence* by Daniel Goleman, Richard Boyatzis, and Annie McKee
- *The High Impact Leader* by Bruce Avolio and Fred Luthans
- *Learned Optimism* by Martin Seligman
- *Optimism* by Helen Keller
- *Resonant Leadership* by Richard Boyatzis and Annie McKee
- *The Student Leadership Challenge* by James M. Kouzes and Barry Z. Posner
- *Happiness: Unlocking the Mysteries of Psychological Wealth* by Ed Diener and Robert Biswas-Diener
- *Authentic Happiness: Using the New Positive Psychology to Realize Your Potential for Lasting Fulfillment* by Martin Seligman

✦ Potential Courses That Relate to This Capacity

- *Business courses*—organizational behavior, leadership or management skills
- *Communication courses*—interpersonal communication, persuasive communication theory, small group communications, organizational communications
- *Leadership courses*

- *Philosophy courses*
- *Psychology courses*—small group dynamics, industrial and organizational psychology, social psychology

Notable Quotes

Leaders with that kind of talent are emotional magnets; people naturally gravitate to them. If you think about the leaders with whom people most want to work in an organization, they probably have this ability to exude upbeat feelings. It's one reason emotionally intelligent leaders attract talented people—for the pleasure of working in their presence.—Daniel Goleman, Richard Boyatzis, and Annie McKee, authors, *Primal Leadership*

Both good and bad moods tend to perpetuate themselves in part because they skew perceptions and memories: When people feel upbeat, they see the positive light in a situation and recall the good things about it, and when they feel bad, they focus on the downside . . . as a result, we naturally prefer being with people who are emotionally positive. In part because they make us feel good.—Daniel Goleman, Richard Boyatzis, and Annie McKee, authors, *Primal Leadership*

I believe that traditional wisdom is incomplete. A composer can have all the talent of Mozart and a passionate desire to succeed, but if he believes he cannot compose music, he will come to nothing. He will not try hard enough. He will give up too soon when the elusive right melody takes too long to materialize.—Martin Seligman, author, *Learned Optimism*

Habits of thinking need not be forever. One of the most significant findings in psychology in the last twenty years is that
individuals can choose the way they think.—Martin Seligman,
author, *Learned Optimism*

Reflection Questions

- Who are the people in your life who best exemplify a
  healthy balance of optimism? What makes you feel this way?
- Where or when are you most optimistic? Who are you working with and what are you working on?
- What environments or individuals bring out the pessimist
  in you?
- How would being more (or less) optimistic improve your
  ability to lead others?
- When you aren't feeling optimistic, do you try to discover
  the positive? If so, how? If not, why not?

CAPACITY 11

Initiative

✦ Initiative Defined

In the *American Heritage Dictionary*, *initiative* is defined as the power or ability to begin or to follow through energetically with a plan or task; enterprise and determination.

Initiative is about wanting and seeking opportunities. Emotionally intelligent leaders understand and take initiative. This means being assertive and seeking out opportunities. Emotionally intelligent leaders must both see the opportunity for change *and* make it happen. Demonstrating initiative means that individuals take action and help the work of the group move forward.

In his video *The Power of Vision* (1991), futurist Joel Barker suggests, "Vision without action is merely a dream. Action without vision just passes time. Vision with action changes the world." Initiative combines thinking about possibilities, imagining a potential direction or action, and making it happen.

✦ Too Much Initiative

Individuals who are too focused on initiative will likely leave others behind. They may get so far ahead of others in the group that it becomes difficult for members to feel included, involved, or engaged. Too much initiative can also be detrimental if the initiative causes harm to others or leads to actions being taken at the expense of others. For instance, leaders who use others for personal gain to "get ahead" risk damaging relationships, losing trust, and threatening friendships along the way. Too much initiative upsets the delicate balance of providing direction and showing the way while also including others and making them feel valued. People do not want to feel bullied or forced into a decision or someone else's course of action. Emotionally intelligent leadership is about process as much as outcome, and too much initiative can destroy the process.

✦ Too Little Initiative

People who lack initiative will struggle when it comes to inspiring others or engaging them in a course of action. In addition, too little initiative on the part of a leader may stall the group's progress. In any group, a lack of initiative easily creates dissonance among people who have different ideas. A common result of too little initiative is apathy. In an organizational context, individuals who lack initiative may also damage relationships with external constituents because of a lack of engagement or follow-through. All organizations have expectations, and leaders with low levels of initiative often have difficulty living up to commitments and obligations.

✦ Student Quotes

I've seen new members to the organization shy away and I've seen them take charge and take on leadership roles. Even just speaking up about a matter being discussed makes me proud.

Students who take initiative tend to be the students who see positive results in a relatively short amount of time.

Initiative comes in many forms. Sometimes it is as simple as doing your homework, but more often it is expressed through stepping up to the plate and taking on a task that no one else will. This can be planning an event, confronting someone, or speaking out for an ideal.

Some leaders take too much initiative and take their project too seriously and become obsessed with perfection while the rest of the group is bullied.

✦ Online Articles and Resources

- http://www.kevinchiu.org—Solving Procrastination: An Application of Flow
- http://www.youtube.com—Mihaly Csikszentmihalyi: Creativity, Fulfillment and Flow
- http://www.Entreprenuer.com—Finding Your Passion
- http://womenentrepreneur.com—Find Your Passion; The Money Will Follow

✦ Suggested Books

- *Flow: The Psychology of Optimal Experience* by Mihaly Csikszentmihalyi
- *Finding Flow: The Psychology of Engagement with Everyday Life* by Mihaly Csikszentmihalyi
- *Spiritual Leaders Who Changed the World: The Essential Handbook of the Past Century of Religion* by Ira Rifkin and Robert Coles
- *Hear Her Voice: Twelve Jewish Women Who Changed the World* by Miriam P. Feinberg and Miriam Klein Shapiro
- *Women Who Changed the World* by Ros Horton and Sally Simmons
- *Girls Who Rocked the World: Heroines from Sacagawea to Sheryl Swoopes (Girls Know Best)* by Amelie Welden and Jerry McCann
- *Girls Who Rocked the World 2: From Harriet Tubman to Mia Hamm (v. 2)* by Michelle Roehm McCann, Jerry McCann, and Michelle Roehm
- *No Opportunity Wasted: Creating a Life List* by Phil Keoghan and Warren Berger

✦ Suggested Films

The following films highlight the capacity of initiative. Some characters may overuse this capacity; others may lack the ability to use it successfully.

- *Patch Adams*
- *Cast Away*
- *Hotel Rwanda*
- *March of the Penguins*
- *The Incredibles*

- *Avatar*
- *Rudy*
- *Schindler's List*
- *The Shawshank Redemption*
- *Chariots of Fire*
- *Miracle*
- *Apollo 13*
- *Gattaca*
- *Saving Private Ryan*
- *Silkwood*

← Potential Courses That Relate to This Capacity

- *Business courses*—organizational behavior, leadership or management skills
- *Career development courses*
- *Communication courses*—interpersonal communication, small group communications
- *Leadership courses*
- *Psychology courses*—small group dynamics, social psychology

← Notable Quotes

Success seems to be connected with action. Successful people keep moving. They make mistakes, but they don't quit.—Conrad Hilton, founder, Hilton Hotels

I would rather regret the things I have done than the things I have not.—Lucille Ball, actress

Even if you're on the right track you'll get run over if you just sit there.—Will Rogers, actor

If opportunity doesn't knock—build a door.—Milton Berle, actor

Problems are only opportunities in work clothes.—Henry Kaiser, American industrialist

The greatest success stories were created by people who recognized a problem and turned it into an opportunity.—Joseph Sugarman, author and entrepreneur

← Reflection Questions

- How does the concept of initiative connect to your definition of leadership?
- Does initiative come naturally or is it a capacity that is more difficult for you to access?
- What is one change you can make to be perceived as a leader with initiative?
- Who do you think of as someone who demonstrates initiative in a positive way? How do others respond to this individual?
- What environments, tasks, and people energize you?
- What does initiative look like when it's all "clicking" for you?

REFERENCE

Barker, J. (1991). *The power of vision* (VHS). United States: Starthrower Distribution.

Empathy

✦ Empathy Defined

In the *American Heritage Dictionary*, *empathy* is defined as identification with and understanding of another's situation, feelings, and motives.

Empathy is about understanding others from their perspective. Emotionally intelligent leadership and, more specifically, the capacity of empathy are about perceiving the emotions of others. When leaders display empathy, they have the opportunity to build healthier relationships, manage difficult situations, and develop trust more effectively. Being empathetic requires an individual to have a high level of self-awareness as well as awareness of others.

✦ Too Much Empathy

At one extreme, those too focused on empathy risk impairing productivity. Too much time spent on other people's feelings, the group process, and ensuring consensus, buy-in, or happiness often results in a lack of progress. Another potential drawback is that an intense focus on empathy may render us unable to make difficult decisions, especially regarding people. We may put off difficult decisions at the expense of organizational need for fear of hurting or offending another person. When we demonstrate too much empathy, others may perceive us as too focused on feelings and not paying enough attention to accomplishing a task or even considering the broader context of the situation. Too much empathy can stall progress and lead to paralysis in organizations and relationships.

✦ Too Little Empathy

People who lack the ability to empathize with others will have a difficult time building genuine relationships. Thus others may feel that their opinion does not matter or their feelings or perspectives are irrelevant. This leaves people imagining that they are simply a means to an end rather than valued members of the group. Those with low levels of empathy also may come off as cold, aloof, or indifferent, which will make it difficult for others to be committed to them. Too little empathy increases the likelihood that decisions or problems will be solved without considering the human dynamic; this often results in ineffective, unproductive, and even unethical decisions.

✦ Student Quotes

Empathy is a requirement in the people business. I don't know that I have encountered someone who was "too empathetic," but I can imagine that the leader could become too bogged down and torn with conflicting emotions of how to deal with such situations while still driving an organization to success.

Empathy allows a leader to understand the lives of those people he or she is leading. The danger of being too empathetic is that an individual can feel so bad for other individuals within a group that they may focus all their time on this as opposed to leading the rest of the group.

All leaders must have the skills to possess empathy so they can read how their actions are affecting not just the entire group but the individuals that comprise that group.

You can't please everyone. Empathy, although important, can be a deterrent to leaders. Empathy can spark a leader to tackle an issue but it can also trap a leader to a single issue. Too much empathy can keep leaders away from practicality.

✦ Online Articles and Resources

- http://newswise.com—Brain Scans Show Children Naturally Prone to Empathy
- http://www.time.com—The Limits of Empathy
- http://findarticles.com—Beyond Video Games: Students Build Empathy Online
- http://www.danielgoleman.info/blog—Three Kinds of Empathy: Cognitive, Emotional, Compassionate
- http://www.youtube.com/watch?v=LGHbbJ5xz3g— President Barack Obama on empathy
- http://video.google.com/—Dev Patnaik on Open Empathy

✦ Suggested Books

- *Creating Harmonious Relationships: A Practical Guide to the Power of True Empathy* by Andrew LeCompte
- *Wisdom of Listening* by Mark Brady
- *Wired to Care: How Companies Prosper When They Create Widespread Empathy* by Dev Patnaik
- *Empathy and Its Development* by Nancy Eisenberg and Janet Strayer
- *Teaching Children Empathy, The Social Emotion: Lessons, Activities and Reproducible Worksheets (K–6) That Teach How to "Step Into Others' Shoes"* by Tonia Caselman
- *The Lost Art of Listening* by Michael P. Nichols
- *A Way of Being* by Carl R. Rogers
- *The Seven Habits of Highly Effective People* by Stephen R. Covey

✦ Suggested Films

The following films highlight the capacity of empathy. Some characters may overuse this capacity; others may lack the ability to use it successfully.

- *My Sister's Keeper*
- *To Kill a Mockingbird*
- *Forrest Gump*
- *Up in the Air*
- *As It Is in Heaven*
- *The Doctor*
- *Hancock*
- *Ice Age* series
- *On the Waterfront*
- *12 Angry Men*

✦ Potential Courses That Relate to This Capacity

- *Business courses*—organizational behavior, leadership or management skills
- *Communication courses*—interpersonal communication, small group communications
- *Leadership courses*
- *Psychology courses*—small group dynamics, social psychology

✦ Notable Quotes

Successful leaders lead with the heart, not just the head. They possess qualities like empathy, compassion and courage. They also have the ability to establish deep, long-term and genuine relationships where others trust them.—Bill George, author, *True North*

Most people do not listen with the intent to understand; they listen with the intent to reply. They're either speaking or preparing to speak. They're filtering everything through their own paradigms, reading their autobiography into other people's lives.—Stephen R. Covey, author, *The Seven Habits of Highly Effective People*

Empathy takes time, and efficiency is for things, not people.—Stephen R. Covey

How far you go in life depends on you being tender with the young, compassionate with the aged, sympathetic with the striving and tolerant of the weak and the strong. Because someday

in life you will have been all of these.—George Washington Carver, American educator and inventor

There's a lot of talk in this country about the federal deficit. But I think we should talk more about our empathy deficit—the ability to put ourselves in someone else's shoes; to see the world through those who are different from us—the child who's hungry, the laid-off steelworker, the immigrant woman cleaning your dorm room.—Barack Obama, forty-fourth president of the United States of America

← Reflection Questions

- How does the concept of empathy relate to how you see yourself?
- How would you assess your ability to be empathetic? When is it easy for you to demonstrate empathy? When is it difficult?
- Think of a time when someone demonstrated empathy toward you. What did they do? How did you feel?
- In what ways do you think empathy is important in a leadership relationship? In what ways can it be inappropriately demonstrated?
- What is one change you can make to be a more empathetic leader?
- Who do you know who models the capacity of empathy in a positive way? How do others respond to this individual?

Citizenship

✦ Citizenship Defined

In the *American Heritage Dictionary*, *citizenship* is defined as the character of an individual viewed as a member of society; behavior in terms of the duties, obligations, and functions of a citizen.

Citizenship is about recognizing and fulfilling your responsibility for others or the group. Emotionally intelligent leaders must be aware of what it means to be a part of something bigger than themselves. An essential component is to fulfill the ethical and moral obligations inherent in the values of the community. As a result, emotionally intelligent leaders know when to give of themselves for the benefit of others and the larger group.

✦ Too Much Citizenship

Those who focus too much on citizenship may become dogmatic and marginalize themselves from others in the group. In addition, they may be seen as individuals who overemphasize the group and wanting to be inclusive to the point that they are rigid and unyielding in the face of ever-changing circumstances. We need to strike a difficult balance between toeing the line of organizational expectations, standards, and obligations and allowing for differences in how this is lived by the members of a group. Too much of a focus on citizenship can mean a loss of self—we should not give so much to others that we lose sight of what is important or what we as individuals can contribute.

← Too Little Citizenship

Those with a low level of citizenship may not understand that they are part of a larger whole. Having too little citizenship makes it difficult to compromise or sacrifice for the greater good. When this happens, others may perceive us as selfish, stubborn, or incapable of giving more than has been asked. Because leaders often set the tone of an organization, when we demonstrate too little citizenship we may be fostering an environment in which others learn that what matters is self-interest or one's own goals. In this case, citizenship does not become a value of the larger organization; instead, what matters is based solely on the ideas and actions of the leader.

← Student Quotes

When members fulfill their duty, the entire aura of the organization is positive. Those not fulfilling duties feel guilty for such, and then rise to the level of responsibility of others.

I believe that there comes a point in an individual's life where they realize that satisfaction does not simply result from making yourself happy. It results from interactions with others and fulfilling their needs. When this occurs a group runs more efficiently.

People are more likely to believe in a person and respect someone who recognizes and fulfills responsibilities to others. People are also more likely to follow such a leader because they believe this person to be someone who truly has an interest in the people.

When someone recognizes and fulfills their responsibilities successfully, that person is respected. It is in one's best interest (if they wish to remain a friend, colleague, etc.) to work at recognizing what people expect out of them.

When someone fulfills their responsibility, a group works well. Oftentimes this person can go unnoticed, in which case it is the leader's responsibility to recognize their efforts and acknowledge them for their good work.

❧ Online Articles and Resources

- http://plato.stanford.edu/entries/citizenship/—Citizenship
- http://www.tandf.co.uk—Citizenship Studies—An Academic Journal
- http://www.queensu.ca/cded/news.html—Citizenship, Democracy and Ethnocultural Diversity Newsletter
- http://www.justiceharvard.org—Justice with Michael Sandel

✦ Suggested Books

- *Take Action! A Guide to Active Citizenship* by Marc Kielburger and Craig Kielburger
- *What Is Citizenship?* by Derek Heater
- *A Brief History of Citizenship* by Derek Heater
- *Citizenship: A Very Short Introduction* by Richard Bellamy
- *Citizenship Papers: Essays* by Wendell Berry
- *Preparing for Citizenship: Teaching Youth to Live Democratically* by Ralph L. Mosher, Robert A. Kenny Jr., and Andrew Garrod
- *The Spirit of Community: The Reinvention of American Society* by Amitai Etzioni
- *The Quickening of America: Rebuilding Our Nation, Remaking Our Lives* by Frances Moore Lappé and Paul Martin DuBois

✦ Suggested Films

The following films highlight the capacity of citizenship. Some characters may overuse this capacity; others may lack the ability to use it successfully.

- *To Kill a Mockingbird*
- *Remember the Titans*
- *Hancock*
- *Hoot*
- *Erin Brockovich*
- *Abraham Lincoln* (A&E Biography)
- *Milton Hershey* (A&E Biography)
- *Eleanor Roosevelt* (A&E Biography)
- *Nelson Mandela* (A&E Biography)
- *Dalai Lama* (A&E Biography)
- *Frederick Douglass* (A&E Biography)

❧ Potential Courses That Relate to This Capacity

- *Philosophy courses*—political philosophy, ethics
- *Psychology courses*—group dynamics, social psychology
- *History courses*—civil rights, American history, democracy studies
- *Political science courses*—political theory, political behavior, peace studies
- *American studies courses*—civil rights, social movements
- *Business courses*—leadership or management skills, organizational behavior
- *Leadership courses*

❧ Notable Quotes

It is not always the same thing to be a good man and a good citizen.—Aristotle, philosopher

Good government is no substitute for self-government.—Mohandas Gandhi, leader of the Indian Nationalist Movement

A nation, as a society, forms a moral person, and every member of it is personally responsible for his society.—Thomas Jefferson, third president of the United States of America

The efforts of the government alone will never be enough. In the end the people must choose and the people must help

themselves.—John F. Kennedy, thirty-fifth president of the United States of America

Let us at all times remember that all American citizens are brothers of a common country, and should dwell together in bonds of fraternal feeling.—Abraham Lincoln, sixteenth president of the United States of America

↤ Reflection Questions

- What does it mean to be a good "citizen" in each of the organizations you are involved in? How do the norms differ across the various organizations?
- Why is the concept of "giving of self" for a greater good difficult for people to do?
- When was the last time you put aside your personal needs for the best interest of the group? What happened as a result?
- How do you motivate others to live up to their commitments and responsibilities to the organization? What works for you?

Inspiration

✦ Inspiration Defined

In the *American Heritage Dictionary*, *inspiration* is defined as stimulation of the mind or emotions to a high level of feeling or activity.

Inspiration is about motivating and moving others toward a shared vision. Being perceived by others as an inspirational individual is an important capacity of emotionally intelligent leadership. Inspiration works through relationships. Effective leadership entails generating feelings of optimism and commitment to organizational goals through individual actions, words, and accomplishments.

✦ Too Much Inspiration

Those who focus too much on inspiration may become too consumed with the vision of the future to think about the present and its realities. Similarly, they may struggle with an inability to implement the ideas being shared. In other words, too much inspiration may also mean a lack of understanding or interest in working toward the future, with little idea of how to help the group get there. This can result in an "all talk and no action" scenario. Eventually this scenario may lead to a loss of trust or disillusionment.

Too Little Inspiration

Those with an inability (or low ability) to inspire may have a difficult time motivating others to work toward a future desired state of being. With too little inspiration, they may lead an organization without a clear sense of purpose or direction. This may result in factions bubbling up or power struggles among members. Too little inspiration may also negatively affect members' interests in being involved or getting others involved—apathy is a common consequence when too little inspiration is demonstrated.

Student Quotes

As a follower I like someone who will give me specific tasks and guide me, but not try to control exactly what I do. I like to be given something specific but still have the creative freedom to do what I think is best. As a follower I like someone who will respect what I do, and truly value my opinion.

I like leaders who are visionary (have good ideas), optimistic (believe something can get done), and encouraging (appreciate the contributions of the different teammates).

I am inspired to follow those who appear confident, educated, and experienced. Also, someone who reaches out to others for their opinions and suggestions and doesn't criticize or belittle those opinions and suggestions.

As a follower, I am inspired by passionate people. People who aren't afraid to put themselves out there, and work for a change. I am inspired by people who are willing to take risks, and those who know that not everything will always work out the way they want it to.

Online Articles and Resources

- http://www.businessweek.com—How to Inspire People Like Obama Does
- http://www.hartwickinstitute.org—Hartwick Leadership Institute
- http://www.americanrhetoric.com—American Rhetoric
- http://content.ksg.harvard.edu—America's Best Leaders
- http://www.time.com/time/time100/leaders/profile/king.html—The Time 100

Suggested Books

- *The Secret Language of Leadership: How Leaders Inspire Action Through Narrative* by Stephen Denning
- *The Leader's Guide to Storytelling: Mastering the Art and Discipline of Business Narrative* by Stephen Denning
- *Squirrel Inc.: A Fable of Leadership Through Storytelling* by Stephen Denning

- *The Handbook of Emotionally Intelligent Leadership: Inspiring Others to Achieve Results* by Daniel A. Feldman
- *Resonant Leadership: Renewing Yourself and Connecting with Others Through Mindfulness, Hope, and Compassion* by Richard E. Boyatzis and Annie McKee
- *Leadership and Performance Beyond Expectations* by Bernard Bass
- *The Leadership Challenge* by James M. Kouzes and Barry Z. Posner

← Suggested Films

The following films highlight the capacity of inspiration. Some characters may overuse this capacity; others may lack the ability to use it successfully.

- *Rudy*
- *Mr. Holland's Opus*
- *Pay It Forward*
- *Rocky*
- *Miracle*
- *The Killing Fields*
- *Braveheart*
- *Erin Brockovich*
- *Lean on Me*
- *Apollo 13*
- *Philadelphia*
- *Glory*
- *Remember the Titans*

✦ Potential Courses That Relate to This Capacity

- *Business courses*—leadership or management skills
- *Communication courses*—interpersonal communication, persuasive communication theory, small group communications, organizational communications
- *History courses*—social history, democratic movements
- *Leadership courses*
- *Psychology courses*—cognitive psychology, social psychology

✦ Notable Quotes

Our chief want is someone who will inspire us to be what we know we could be.—Ralph Waldo Emerson, poet

Leaders establish the vision for the future and set the strategy for getting there; they cause change. They motivate and inspire others to go in the right direction and they, along with everyone else, sacrifice to get there.—John Kotter, author, *Leading Change*

People are not lazy. They simply have impotent goals—that is, goals that do not inspire them.—Anthony Robbins, motivational speaker

Good actions give strength to ourselves and inspire good actions in others.—Plato, philosopher

Transformational leaders behave in ways that motivate and inspire those around them by providing meaning and challenge to their followers' work. Team spirit is aroused. Enthusiasm and optimism are displayed. Leaders get followers involved in envisioning attractive future states; they create clearly communicated expectations that followers want to meet and also demonstrate commitment to goals and the shared vision.—Bernard Bass, leadership scholar

✦ Reflection Questions

- What inspires you? Create a list that includes ideas, values, and issues.
- When have you inspired someone? What did you do to make this happen? What were the results?
- What happens in an organization or group when the leader is seen as inspiring?
- Who is someone that you know who inspires you? In what ways?
- How do you know when you've been inspired? Inspired others?
- Think about what's going on in today's world. Who do you see playing an inspirational role? What are they doing?

Influence

✦ Influence Defined

In the *American Heritage Dictionary*, *influence* is defined as power to sway or affect based on prestige, wealth, ability, or position.

Influence is about demonstrating skills of persuasion. Emotionally intelligent leaders have the ability to persuade others with information, ideas, emotion, behavior, and a strong commitment to organizational values and purpose. They involve others to engage in a process of mutual exploration and action.

✦ Too Much Influence

A person who influences too much may be seen by others as bossy, demanding, or unwilling to listen to others' ideas—or even incapable of doing so. The consequences of too much influence are many: alienating others, causing conflict, becoming the sole person in an organization committed to a course of action, and so forth. Those who wield too much influence fail to create the space for others to shine and develop. If an organization or group becomes overly dependent on one influential person, its long-term success may suffer. Of course, one other serious challenge associated with too much influence is that if the person is promoting an unethical course of action or actions detrimental to others, few will be willing or able to intervene.

⬅ Too Little Influence

Individuals lacking the ability to influence struggle with a core skill of leadership. Too little influence means that they have difficulty helping others see a particular point of view. It is also difficult to encourage or motivate others to do something they didn't think was possible. Individuals influence one another in many ways, including through their own words and actions. Influence may also be demonstrated through relationships and visions of a better future. Those who lack ability in any of these forms of influence will have a challenging time getting others to follow or join in an effort. In the end, people with too little influence may find they are doing a lot of the work all by themselves.

⬅ Student Quotes

I have a lot more respect for someone who can take the ideas of others and use them, as opposed to only doing it one way.

[Influence is] a style that is both flash and substance. If someone can stand and keep my attention while providing me with a purpose, then I will go with them until the project is complete.

Direction and energy are what capture me; if a leader has that
I will follow.

I like a leader who is compassionate, takes the project seriously,
and has passion for what needs to be done.

← Online Articles and Resources

- http://www.businessweek.com—Leadership: Intentional Influence
- http://www.influenceatwork.com—Influence at Work
- http://wakalix.com/booknotes/Cialdini_interview.html—An Interview with Robert B. Cialdini
- http://www.insideinfluence.com—Inside Influence Report

← Suggested Books

- *How to Win Friends and Influence People* by Dale Carnegie
- *Influence: The Psychology of Persuasion* by Robert B. Cialdini
- *Influence: Science and Practice* by Robert B. Cialdini
- *Yes! 50 Scientifically Proven Ways to Be Persuasive* by Robert B. Cialdini
- *Relational Intelligence: How Leaders Can Expand Their Influence Through a New Way of Being Smart* by Steve Saccone
- *The Tipping Point: How Little Things Can Make a Big Difference* by Malcolm Gladwell
- *Talk Less, Say More: Three Habits to Influence Others and Make Things Happen* by Connie Dieken
- *Influence: Gaining Commitment, Getting Results* by Center for Creative Leadership, David Baldwin, and Curt Grayson

- *Influence Without Authority* by Allan R. Cohen and David L. Bradford
- *Persuasive Messages: The Process of Influence* by William Benoit and Pamela Benoit

✦ Suggested Films

The following films highlight the capacity of influence. Some characters may overuse this capacity; others may lack the ability to use it successfully.

- *Dead Poets Society*
- *The Shawshank Redemption*
- *Mad Hot Ballroom*
- *School of Rock*
- *Star Wars* series
- *The Matrix*
- *Apollo 13*
- *Harry Potter* series
- *Glory*
- *Braveheart*
- *Remember the Titans*
- *Avatar*

✦ Potential Courses That Relate to This Capacity

- *Business courses*—leadership or management skills
- *Communication courses*—interpersonal communication, persuasive communication theory, small group communications, organizational communications
- *Leadership courses*
- *Psychology courses*—small group dynamics, industrial and organizational psychology, social psychology

✦ Notable Quotes

Leadership is a process whereby an individual influences a group of individuals to achieve a common goal.—Peter Northouse, author, *Leadership: Theory and Practice*

Clearly the leader who commands compelling causes has an extraordinary potential influence over followers. Followers armed by moral inspiration, mobilized and purposeful, become zealots and leaders in their own right.—James MacGregor Burns, author, *Leadership*

People change what they do less because they are given *analysis* that shifts their *thinking* than because they are *shown* a truth that influences their *feelings*.—John Kotter, author, *The Heart of Change*

Leaders not only influence followers but are under their influence as well.—Ron Heifetz, author, *Leadership Without Easy Answers*

Indicators of a leader's powers of influence range from finding just the right appeal for a given listener to knowing how to build buy-in from key people and a network of support for an initiative. Leaders adept in influence are persuasive and engaging when they address a group.—Daniel Goleman, Richard E. Boyatzis, and Annie McKee, authors, *Primal Leadership*

Example is not the main thing in influencing others. It is the only thing.—Albert Schweitzer, philosopher

✦ Reflection Questions

- In what ways do you influence others? Describe how you've been successful in a variety of ways.
- What type of leaders influence you to follow? What are their attributes?
- What aspects of your personality will enhance your ability to influence others? Which will limit your ability to influence others?
- Who do you believe is talented at influencing others? What do they do well? What aspects of their personality do you think others find compelling?

CAPACITY 16

Coaching

✦ Coaching Defined

In the *American Heritage Dictionary*, the verb *coach* is defined as to give instruction or advice . . . in the capacity of a coach; instruct.

Coaching is about helping others enhance their skills and abilities. Emotionally intelligent leaders know that they cannot do everything themselves; they need others to become a part of the endeavor. Coaching is about intentionally helping others demonstrate their talent; it requires the emotionally intelligent leader to prioritize how time is spent to foster the development of others in the group—not just themselves.

✦ Too Much Coaching

Those focused too much on coaching may find themselves with groups who cannot function when they are not present. Coaching is important, but the purpose should be to prepare others to assume a leadership role or carry out a set of responsibilities, not to simply make them dependent. Those who rely too much on coaching may believe they must be involved in every decision or action taken by the group. When done well, coaching empowers others to demonstrate their talents and skills. To make this happen, those who coach must give others opportunities to grow and develop, then allow them to venture out on their own.

Too Little Coaching

Individuals who lack the ability to coach others miss out on capitalizing on a fundamental attribute of effective leadership. After all, leadership is about achieving a mutually desirable goal through a process of coming together. For a goal to be shared, the coach needs to create space for others to be involved in meaningful ways, which takes time. Individuals who do not take the time to build leadership capacity in others may find themselves on an island—disconnected from the larger group, working alone, and lacking a shared vision for a better future. Without sharing their knowledge through coaching, leaders find they have no one to delegate to and no one who can help in a supportive, knowledgeable way.

Student Quotes

Whenever someone has helped me develop a skill, they show me exactly what I am doing and then show me how the task needs to be accomplished. The person then coaches and aids while I try to mimic their actions.

When I first started playing hockey I could not (for the life of me) skate. My coach spent time with me, showing me how, and being there to support me . . . Thanks to him, I went on to play another 13 years and get varsity letters for it.

I meet with my advisor every Monday. We reflect on incidents that occurred throughout the week. I have had him remind me to keep my tone in check when talking to students so I do not let aggravation or frustration show. That is hard to control . . . it shows in your voice and body language.

The first publisher I worked for often gave me tips and advice on how to improve my writing skills. He did so in a way that made me [confident] in my ability to produce a better product for him. He never made me feel incompetent. I felt more like a student, learning from a seasoned veteran who cared enough to share his tips.

← Online Articles and Resources

- http://blogs.wsj.com—Executive Coaching—Worth the Money?
- http://www.blessingwhite.com—The Coaching Conundrum Report
- http://www.coachfederation.org—International Coach Federation
- http://blogs.harvardbusiness.org/goldsmith—Marshall Goldsmith: Ask the Coach
- http://blogs.harvardbusiness.org/goldsmith—Center for Executive Coaching Blog

- http://hbswk.hbs.edu/archive/4853.html—What an Executive Coach Can Do for You
- http://www.fastcompany.com/resources/learning/ bolt/041006.html—Coaching: The Fad That Won't Go Away

✦ Suggested Books

- *The Art and Practice of Leadership Coaching: 50 Top Executive Coaches Reveal Their Secrets* by Howard Morgan, Phil Harkins, and Marshall Goldsmith
- *The Successful Coach: Insider Secrets to Becoming a Top Coach* by Terri Levine, Larina Kase, and Joe Vitale
- *Coaching in Organizations: Best Coaching Practices from The Ken Blanchard Companies* by Madeleine Homan and Linda J. Miller
- *Reach for the Summit* by Pat Summitt
- *Wooden on Leadership: How to Create a Winning Organization* by John Wooden
- *They Call Me Coach* by John Wooden
- *Coaching People: Expert Solutions to Everyday Challenges* by Harvard Business School Press
- *Coaching Questions: A Coach's Guide to Powerful Asking Skills* by Tony Stoltzfus
- *The Portable Coach: 28 Surefire Strategies for Business and Personal Success* by Thomas Leonard

✦ Suggested Films

The following films highlight the capacity of coaching. Some characters may overuse this capacity; others may lack the ability to use it successfully.

- *Searching for Bobby Fischer*
- *Miracle*
- *Lords of Dogtown*
- *Hoosiers*
- *Coach Carter*
- *Friday Night Lights*
- *Karate Kid*
- *Remember the Titans*
- *Dead Poets Society*
- *Million Dollar Baby*
- *School of Rock*
- *Born into Brothels*
- *Mad Hot Ballroom*

Potential Courses That Relate to This Capacity

- *Business courses*—organizational behavior, leadership or management skills
- *Communication courses*—interpersonal communication, persuasive communication theory, small group communications
- *Leadership courses*
- *Psychology courses*—small group dynamics, industrial and organizational psychology, social psychology, sports psychology

Notable Quotes

Make sure that team members know they are working with you, not for you.—John Wooden, former UCLA basketball coach

A coach is someone who can give correction without causing resentment.—John Wooden, former UCLA basketball coach

Our chief want in life is somebody who makes us do what we can.—Ralph Waldo Emerson, philosopher and poet

Coaching is a profession of love. You can't coach people unless you love them.—Eddie Robinson, football coach, Grambling State University

Learning is a willingness to let one's ability and attitude to change in response to new ideas, information and experiences.—Peter Vaill, leadership scholar

She taught me that it's OK to let down your guard and allow your players to get to know you. They don't care how much you know until they know how much you care.—Pat Summitt, University of Tennessee women's basketball coach

Over the long run, superior performance depends on superior learning.—Peter Senge, author, *The Fifth Discipline: The Art and Practice of the Learning Organization*

← Reflection Questions

- Do you have a natural ability to coach others? How do you know this?

- In what ways are you interested in helping others succeed?
- What are attributes of great mentors, teachers, athletic coaches, pastors, and so on with whom you have worked? What was their approach to coaching you?
- How is a coach different from a mentor?
- Who are people who you know who could coach? Younger members of your organization(s)? High school students? Friends or relatives?

Change Agent

✦ Change Agent Defined

In the *American Heritage Dictionary*, *change* is defined as to cause to be different.

Being a change agent is about seeking out and working with others to move in new directions. As change agents, emotionally intelligent leaders look for opportunities for improvement or innovation—they think about possibilities and are future oriented. They see how change may benefit one person, an organization, or a whole community, and work to make this change happen.

✦ Too Much Change Agent

Too much focus on being a change agent can be disruptive and even damaging—to individuals, relationships, projects, and organizations. At one extreme, those focused too much on being a change agent may struggle against the constant challenges facing any organization or group. There are so many opportunities for development and growth that they may become consumed with the tasks and "stuff" of organizational life and lose sight of the human element. In addition, they may isolate themselves if the changes are too frequent and challenging. Leadership scholars Ron Heifetz and Martin Linsky call these "adaptive challenges" and suggest, "Adaptive work creates risk, conflict, and instability because addressing the issues underlying adaptive problems may involve upending deep and entrenched norms. Thus, leadership requires disturbing people—but at a rate they can absorb" (Heifetz & Linsky, 2002, p. 20).

← Too Little Change Agent

Individuals who are content with the status quo may find themselves (and their organization or group) lacking relevance as the environment changes. As needs or challenges arise, those who have too little focus on being a change agent may miss opportunities for innovation or new experiences. Individuals with too little focus on being a change agent may lack either the vision for seeing what is possible or the ability to implement a change. Leaders with little vision for a better future will have a difficult time energizing organizational members to work in a common direction. Those individuals who have the ability to energize the group but lack the follow-through (making the vision a reality) will be challenged as well.

← Student Quotes

Change doesn't happen on its own. People must be involved to make changes within an organization. In order for these changes to be effective there must be a united front or opinion regarding the direction of the change, and this united front cannot form unless a leader is there to guide the discussion and actions of the group.

In order for change to happen, someone has to be a leader—every revolution in history has had a leader, and the same is necessary in micro-scale revolutions as well.

Many times, a change that needs to be made requires someone to step up and take a stand for what is right. A lot of people are afraid to initiate changes because they do not want people to fail. It takes a true leader to initiate a change and get support.

Leadership is the vehicle that combines the passions and desires, overcoming the fears and confusion of the group towards a shared vision.

Change only happens through the influence of great leaders who get others excited about the change.

Online Articles and Resources

- http://www.Inc.com—Leading Change—Creating an Organization That Lives Change
- http://www.esi-intl.com—Leading Change: A Model by John Kotter
- http://www.johnkotter.com—The personal website of John Kotter
- http://www.fastcompany.com—Leading Change blog
- http://changingminds.org—Change Management
- http://www.change-management-blog.com—Change Management Blog

✦ Suggested Books

- *Leading Change* by John P. Kotter
- *Our Iceberg Is Melting: Changing and Succeeding Under Any Conditions* by John Kotter, Holger Rathgeber, Peter Mueller, and Spencer Johnson
- *The Heart of Change: Real-Life Stories of How People Change Their Organizations* by John P. Kotter and Dan S. Cohen
- *The Dance of Change: The Challenges to Sustaining Momentum in Learning Organizations* by Peter M. Senge, Art Kleiner, Charlotte Roberts, and George Roth
- *Managing Change and Transition* by Richard Luecke and Harvard Business School Press
- *Who Killed Change?: Solving the Mystery of Leading People Through Change* by Ken Blanchard
- *Immunity to Change: How to Overcome It and Unlock the Potential in Yourself and Your Organization* by Robert Kegan and Lisa Laskow Lahey
- *Who Moved My Cheese?: An Amazing Way to Deal with Change in Your Work and in Your Life* by Spencer Johnson and Kenneth Blanchard
- *All Hat and No Cattle: Shaking up the System and Making a Difference at Work* by Chris Turner

✦ Suggested Films

The following films highlight the capacity of change agent. Some characters may overuse this capacity; others may lack the ability to use it successfully.

- *The Firm*
- *Malcolm X*
- *An Inconvenient Truth*
- *Erin Brockovich*
- *Sitting Bull* (A&E Biography)

- *Eleanor Roosevelt* (A&E Biography)
- *Joan of Arc* (A&E Biography)
- *Bill Gates* (A&E Biography)
- *Amelia Earhart* (A&E Biography)
- *Jackie Robinson* (A&E Biography)

⬅ Potential Courses That Relate to This Capacity

- *Business courses*—organizational behavior, leadership or management skills
- *Communication courses*—interpersonal communication, small group communications
- *Leadership courses*
- *Political science*—contemporary issues, civil rights
- *Psychology courses*—small group dynamics, social psychology
- *Women's studies*

⬅ Notable Quotes

There is nothing wrong with change, if it is in the right direction.—Winston Churchill, former British prime minister

Leadership is a relationship, founded on trust and confidence. Without trust and confidence, people don't take risks. Without risks, there's no change. Without change, organizations and movements die. Whatever the challenge, all involve a change from the status quo.—Kouzes and Posner, authors, *The Leadership Challenge*

By far the biggest mistake people make when trying to change organizations is to plunge ahead without establishing a high

enough sense of urgency in fellow managers and employees.—
John Kotter, author, *Leading Change*

The single most important message of this book is very simple.
People change what they do less because they are given analysis
that shifts their thinking than because they are shown a truth that
influences their feelings.—John Kotter, author, *The Heart of Change*

← Reflection Questions

- Do you naturally "see" possibilities for your organization?
  How do you see the steps it will take to make the
  possibilities a reality?
- What are common pitfalls a person interested in facilitating
  change will face?
- Have you led a change initiative in an organization?
  What strengths did you bring to the endeavor? What
  challenged you?
- Why is it important to include others in setting the course
  for your organization?
- Reflect on a time you witnessed a change that failed. What
  happened? Why did it not take root?

REFERENCE

Heifetz, R. A., & Linsky, M. (2002). *Leadership on the line*. Cambridge, MA:
Harvard Business Review.

Conflict Management

✦ Conflict Management Defined

In the *American Heritage Dictionary*, *conflict* is defined as a state of disharmony between incompatible or antithetical persons, ideas, or interests; a clash.

Conflict management is about identifying and resolving problems and contentious issues with others. Emotionally intelligent leaders understand that conflict is part of any leadership experience. When managed effectively, conflict can foster great innovation. At times conflict is overt and may involve anger, raised voices, or high levels of frustration. Other times conflict is below the surface and shows itself only through cliques, side conversations, and apathy. Emotionally intelligent leaders are aware of these dynamics and work to manage them.

✦ Too Much Conflict Management

Those too focused on conflict management may find themselves unable to move forward due to excessive concern for the feelings of others or the issues that are challenging a group. Sometimes this level of concern is based on fear of conflict or an uncertainty of how to deal with conflict. Conflict is a naturally occurring phenomenon in all human interactions; it can lead to healthy individual and group development. An overemphasis on resolving differences may stall progress and cause organizations and individuals to lose momentum. Finally, leaders who focus too heavily on conflict management may make large issues out of small ones and ultimately increase the level of conflict in the group.

Too Little Conflict Management

Individuals who lack the ability to navigate conflict will have a difficult time leading others. Conflict is present in all organizations, and the inability to help others navigate differences will hinder their ability to move forward and help the work of the group proceed. In addition, a lack of conflict management skills results in unresolved issues among members. These issues may stall progress, create apathy, and cause mistrust among members because it is difficult for the group to feel a true sense of team to proceed in the best way possible.

Student Quotes

[Conflict management means] being agreeable, understanding, and willing to devote time and attention to generating alternatives and avenues for reaching those people that may be creating conflict. Managing conflict also means being willing to assume the negative feedback that may be concomitant with an environment where conflict exists.

[Conflict management means] being able to identify the problem, not just the "symptoms" of the problem, and developing different methods to solve the problem. Always listen to everyone's ideas, because sometimes the most ridiculous sounding idea ends up being the savior.

You must utilize all of the resources of each member of the team. When a person has something to offer and feels that his or her assets are not being utilized, they will become disengaged. Conflict management works the same way. You must first acknowledge the mutual worth of each member, maintain [a] positive [attitude], and acknowledge fault on both parts. At that point you can then start working toward a solution.

To be effective at managing conflict, one must be neutral and willing to hear both sides of the story. I have experienced this through peer mediation. It's difficult at times; however, I know that there must be common ground to solve conflict.

There was a roommate conflict and one wanted to move out. That roommate approached me and we decided to have a discussion with our other roommate. The open communication among the three of us was very important to getting to the root of the problem. The ability to compromise was essential to coming up with a solution.

← Online Articles and Resources

- http://www.pon.org/catalog/index.php—Program on Negotiation at Harvard Law School Clearinghouse

- http://www.mediate.com/articles/rashidJ1.cfm—Leadership Development: Conflict Management for College Student Leaders
- http://disputeresolution.ohio.gov—Choosing a Conflict Management Style
- http://www.kilmann.com/conflict.html—Thomas-Kilmann Conflict MODE Instrument

✦ Suggested Books

- *Getting to Yes* by Bruce M. Patton, William L. Ury, and Roger Fisher
- *Beyond Reason: Using Emotions as You Negotiate* by Roger Fisher and Daniel Shapiro
- *Difficult Conversations: How to Discuss What Matters Most* by Douglas Stone, Bruce Patton, Sheila Heen, and Roger Fisher
- *The Coward's Guide to Conflict: Empowering Solutions for Those Who Would Rather Run Than Fight* by Tim Ursiny
- *Conflict Management, Third Edition: Resolving Disagreements in the Workplace* (Crisp Fifty-Minute Books) by Herbert S. Kindler
- *Managing Conflict with Your Boss* by Center for Creative Leadership, Davida Sharpe, and Elinor Johnson
- *Fierce Conversations: Achieving Success at Work and in Life, One Conversation at a Time* by Susan Scott

✦ Suggested Films

The following films highlight the capacity of conflict management. Some characters may overuse this capacity; others may lack the ability to use it successfully.

- *Ralph Bunche: An American Odyssey*
- *12 Angry Men*
- *Hotel Rwanda*
- *Schindler's List*
- *Glory*
- *Gandhi*
- *1776*
- *War of the Roses*
- *13 Days*
- *Abraham Lincoln* (A&E Biography)
- *Nelson Mandela* (A&E Biography)

Potential Courses That Relate to This Capacity

- *Business courses*—organizational behavior, leadership or management skills
- *Communication courses*—interpersonal communication, persuasive communication theory, small group communications, organizational communications
- *Leadership courses*
- *Psychology courses*—small group dynamics, industrial and organizational psychology, social psychology

Notable Quotes

You gain strength, courage and confidence by every experience in which you must stop and look fear in the face.—Eleanor Roosevelt, former First Lady of the United States

Never in this world can hatred be stilled by hatred; it will be stilled only by non-hatred; this is the law eternal.—Siddhartha Gautama, founder of Buddhism

If we manage conflict constructively, we harness its energy for creativity and development.—Kenneth Kaye, author

When conflict becomes a win-lose contest in our minds, we immediately try to win.—Thomas Crum, author and presenter

Work on developing a cooperative relationship, so when conflict comes, you believe you are allies.—Dean Tjosvold, director of the Hong Kong Cooperative Learning Center

Smooth seas do not make skillful sailors.—African proverb

Out beyond ideas of rightdoing and wrongdoing, there is a field. I will meet you there.—Rumi, poet and philosopher

Everything that irritates us about others can lead us to an understanding of ourselves.—Carl Jung, psychologist

✦ Reflection Questions

- What is your approach to conflict management?
- How would you evaluate your effectiveness when working through conflict?
- How does it feel to have unresolved conflict with others in an organization or group? How have you seen this impact the group?
- In your experience, who is someone close to you who effectively manages conflict? What makes this person successful at doing so?

CAPACITY 19

Developing Relationships

❧ Developing Relationships Defined

In the *American Heritage Dictionary*, a *relationship* is defined as a particular type of connection existing between people related to or having dealings with each other.

Developing relationships is about creating connections between, among, and with people. Developing relationships is a skill as well as a mind-set. This capacity requires emotionally intelligent leaders to build relationships and create a sense of trust and mutual interest. Simply put, individuals, groups, and organizations are stronger, smarter, and more effective when they are rooted in and facilitate positive relationships.

❧ Too Much Developing Relationships

Individuals who focus too much of their time and energy developing relationships may lose sight of the tasks and deadlines of the group. They may spend so much time developing relationships that they may not have enough time for other things, or even forget that work has to get done. Because connecting with others is a primary source of energy for some people, they may find they have little energy left for the work at hand. Interestingly, a person who leads through relationships may (quite innocently) develop cliques or "in" and "out" groups within the organization. In addition, when serving in an official leadership capacity, those with too much focus on developing relationships may choose to promote, support, or appoint friends who may not be the best for the job. This can lead to alienating others and diminishing their trust.

✦ Too Little Developing Relationships

As Dr. Susan Komives writes in the foreword of our book *Emotionally Intelligent Leadership: A Guide for College Students* (2008), "It's all about relationships." In the realm of leadership, relationships are, in many cases, the fuel that drives an organization. With too little skill in developing relationships, individuals lose the ability to get work done through and with others. Individuals who lack this skill may find themselves the only ones doing the work, because they haven't connected others with the vision or task at hand. Communication, phone calls, texts, and emails may go unanswered. Finally, those who are perceived to demonstrate too little capacity for developing relationships may be seen as uncaring or self-centered.

✦ Student Quotes

It's very simple—just getting involved can do so much. Almost every relationship I have made thus far in college has been due to getting to know someone through initial contact or by getting involved.

It is critical to ask questions and listen. By asking questions and carefully listening an individual can quickly find out another's interests, passions, and feelings. This simple process is the beginning to building new relationships.

Find common ground, like similar experiences, use that to comfortably interact, then begin opening up more and seeing where it goes.

To build a relationship I simply start by talking to people about things we have in common such as work or classes. For me in particular this is very hard. I feel that I am a shy person around people I don't know well.

I use my sense of humor and people warm to me quite well. I am comfortable with being funny and outgoing.

Online Articles and Resources

- http://hbr.org/product/how-leaders-create-and-use-networks/an/R0701C-PDF-ENG—*Harvard Business Review*—How Leaders Create and Use Networks
- www.businessknowhow.com/tips/networking—Ten Tips for Successful Business Networking
- http://www.10e20.com/blog/2009/04/30/social-networking-101-basic-tips-for-online-and-offline-social-networking/—Social Networking 101: Basic Tips for Online and Offline Social Networking

← Suggested Books

- *Whale Done!: The Power of Positive Relationships* by Kenneth Blanchard, Thad Lacinak, Chuck Tompkins, and Jim Ballard
- *Becoming a Resonant Leader: Develop Your Emotional Intelligence, Renew Your Relationships, Sustain Your Effectiveness* by Richard E. Boyatzis, Fran Johnston, and Annie McKee
- *Transformational Leadership* by Bernard M. Bass and Ronald E. Riggio
- *Transforming Leadership* by James MacGregor Burns
- *The Leadership Challenge* by James M. Kouzes and Barry Z. Posner
- *Improving Leadership Effectiveness: The Leader Match Concept* by Fred Fiedler, Martin Chemers, and Linda Mahar

← Suggested Films

The following films highlight the capacity of developing relationships. Some characters may overuse this capacity; others may lack the ability to use it successfully.

- *Fried Green Tomatoes*
- *Terms of Endearment*
- *Sleepless in Seattle*
- *Good Will Hunting*
- *Up in the Air*
- *Forrest Gump*
- *Miracle*
- *Avatar*
- *Rudy*
- *The Shawshank Redemption*
- *Dead Man Walking*
- *Powder*

- *Mean Girls*
- *Beaches*

✦ Potential Courses That Relate to This Capacity

- *Business courses*—organizational behavior, leadership or management skills
- *Communication courses*—interpersonal communication, persuasive communication theory, small group communications, organizational communications
- *Leadership courses*
- *Psychology courses*—small group dynamics, industrial and organizational psychology, social psychology

✦ Notable Quotes

Whenever you're in conflict with someone, there is one factor that can make the difference between damaging your relationship and deepening it. That factor is attitude.—William James, psychologist and philosopher

Friendship is born at that moment when one person says to another, "What! You too? I thought I was the only one."—C. S. Lewis, author, *Chronicles of Narnia*

Well, I've been a self-esteem expert for years and there's two things that build self-esteem. One is quality of relationships, where you feel lovable and you're making a difference in the lives of others. And the other is achieving things.—Jack Canfield, author, *Chicken Soup for the Soul*

The essence of any religion lies solely in the answer to the question: why do I exist, and what is my relationship to the infinite universe that surrounds me?—Leo Tolstoy, author, *War and Peace*

All I can say is the most important part of being in a relationship is that you love the person for who they are.—Liv Tyler, actress

← Reflection Questions

- What are the ingredients for developing a truly meaningful relationship? What does it take to maintain these relationships?
- How do you develop a trusting relationship? How do you know when trust exists?
- What aspects of your character make it difficult for others to be in relationship with you?
- What does it take for you to effectively develop relationships? How easy or difficult is it for you to do this?
- Does an individual need to be outgoing to excel at this capacity? What strategies can a more quiet individual use to connect with others?

REFERENCE

Shankman, M. L., & Allen, S. J. (2008). *Emotionally intelligent leadership: A guide for college students.* San Francisco: Jossey-Bass.

Teamwork

✦ Teamwork Defined

In the *American Heritage Dictionary*, *teamwork* is defined as cooperative effort by the members of a group or team to achieve a common goal.

Teamwork is about working effectively with others in a group. Emotionally intelligent leaders know how to work with others to bring out the best in each team member. By facilitating good communication, creating shared purpose, clarifying roles, and facilitating results, emotionally intelligent leaders foster group cohesion and develop a true sense of togetherness that leads to desired results.

✦ Too Much Teamwork

Those too focused on teamwork risk losing productivity and credibility. If too much time is spent on group process (such as ensuring consensus, buy-in, or happiness), the result may be a group that does not see progress. Too much emphasis on

131

teamwork may diminish the importance of action and results. Because so much time and energy gets spent on creating a sense of team, those involved may feel this leader doesn't care enough about getting results—creating a lack of credibility. Another potential drawback is that an intense focus on team may stifle individual strengths and contributions. Groupthink, or the pressure to blend into the larger group, results when a person pushes too hard to get everyone to conform.

Too Little Teamwork

Individuals who do not focus on building a sense of team will likely find themselves with numerous challenges. Typically, if people are involved in a group or organization that lacks cohesion, they will experience a lack of commitment to a vision and purpose for the group. With too little teamwork, team members tend not to trust each other—or even like each other. Thus, they will hardly work well together. In this scenario, those who demonstrate too little teamwork will find themselves doing the majority of the work alone. Another consequence of too little teamwork is that the likelihood for conflict is increased, so leaders may end up dealing more with internal strife than with the work of the organization.

Student Quotes

People must understand that each member has valuable input for the group. It is also important for the team to not come to decisions too quickly or too slowly. It is important to examine numerous possibilities to ensure that the action taken is one of the best options. A team must believe in each of its members and every member must contribute for a team to succeed.

The real key to a successful team is having a firm understanding of the goal of the group, and then knowing how each individual can most effectively contribute to the achievement of this goal.

A team must all be willing to help. If you have one person who doesn't care, it can bring down the morale of the entire team. Everyone should respect each other's thoughts and opinions even if they do not share them.

← Online Articles or Resources

- http://www.businessballs.com—Bruce Tuckman's Forming, Storming, Norming, Performing Model
- http://www.belbin.com—Belbin Team Role Theory
- http://www.youtube.com—Belbin Team Roles Training Bite
- http://www.youtube.com—Belbin Team Roles—An Introduction
- http://www.businessweek.com—Surprising Pitfalls of Teamwork Training
- http://www.wilderdom.com/games—Wilderdom
- http://www.stsintl.com/index.html—Simulation Training Systems

← Suggested Books

- *The Five Dysfunctions of a Team: A Leadership Fable* by Patrick Lencioni
- *Overcoming the Five Dysfunctions of a Team* by Patrick Lencioni

- *The Wisdom of Teams: Creating a High Performance Organization* by Jon R. Katzenbach and Douglas K. Smith
- *The 17 Essential Qualities of a Team Player: Becoming the Kind of Person Every Team Wants* by John C. Maxwell
- *Team of Rivals* by Doris Kearns Goodwin
- *When Teams Work Best: 6,000 Team Members and Leaders Tell What It Takes to Succeed* by Frank M. J. LaFasto and Carl E. Larson
- *Leading Teams: Setting the Stage for Great Performances* by J. Richard Hackman
- *Groups That Work (and Those That Don't): Creating Conditions for Effective Teamwork* by J. Richard Hackman

✦ Suggested Films

The following films highlight the capacity of teamwork. Some characters may overuse this capacity; others may lack the ability to use it successfully.

- *Miracle*
- *Remember the Titans*
- *Rudy*
- *White Squall*
- *The Great Debaters*
- *Facing the Giants*
- *Any Given Sunday*
- *Hoosiers*
- *A League of Their Own*
- *Eight Men Out*
- *Ocean's 11*
- *The Blind Side*

✦ Potential Courses That Relate to This Capacity

- *Business courses*—organizational behavior, leadership or management skills
- *Communication courses*—interpersonal communication, persuasive communication theory, small group communications, organizational communications
- *Leadership courses*
- *Psychology courses*—small group dynamics, industrial and organizational psychology, social psychology
- *Sociology courses*—community development, small group dynamics

✦ Notable Quotes

Trust lies at the heart of a functioning, cohesive team. Without it, teamwork is all but impossible.—Patrick Lencioni, author, *The Five Dysfunctions of a Team*

All great relationships, the ones that last over time, require productive conflict in order to grow. This is true in marriage, parenthood, friendship, and certainly business.—Patrick Lencioni, author, *The Five Dysfunctions of a Team*

By choosing the team path instead of the working group, people commit to take the risks of conflict, joint work-products, and collective action necessary to build a common purpose, set of goals, approach, and mutual accountability.—Jon R. Katzenbach and Douglas K. Smith, authors, *The Wisdom of Teams*

When a team outgrows individual performance and learns team confidence, excellence becomes a reality.—Joe Paterno, football coach, Pennsylvania State University

← Reflection Questions

- In your experience, who in your life has done the best job of building a team that you participated in? What did he or she do?
- What behaviors of teammates drain or exhaust you? What is your usual response?
- How do you make it difficult for others to be on a team with you?
- What role do you generally play on a team? What strengths to you bring to this role?
- When have you been part of an effective team? Describe the experience. How did you feel? What did you do? What were the results?

CAPACITY 21

Capitalizing on Difference

✦ Capitalizing on Difference Defined

In the *American Heritage Dictionary*, *difference* is defined as the quality or condition of being unlike or dissimilar.

Capitalizing on difference is about building on assets that stem from differences among people. Capitalizing on difference suggests that differences are seen as adding benefits, not as the source of barriers. Difference may mean race, socioeconomic status, religion, sexual orientation, or gender as well as ability, personality, or philosophy. When capitalized on, these differences create a larger perspective—a more inclusive view. Emotionally intelligent leaders use these differences as an opportunity to help others grow, develop, and ultimately capitalize on them.

✦ Too Much Capitalizing on Difference

Individuals who are too focused on capitalizing on difference may be challenged by trying to please all parties. They may be so determined to accommodate everyone that they satisfy no one.

In addition, they may lose sight of the real objective at hand and become bogged down in the group's process. When process takes precedence over outcome, groups easily get overly concerned with themselves. This self-centeredness of the group rarely yields positive outcomes. Moreover, these individuals may create an environment so focused on difference that the group loses sight of both its similarities and the need to compromise.

✦ Too Little Capitalizing on Difference

Those who lack the ability to capitalize on difference will miss out on opportunities to see the bigger picture. Differing perspectives help leaders see a more holistic picture, which they will miss if they recognize only one perspective. As a result, these individuals and their groups may not choose a course of action that best suits the context. In addition, individuals who fail to create an environment in which differences are valued will close themselves off from valuable resources that could assist the effort, organization, or group. Individual members may feel they are not important or valued by the person and/or the organization. When this happens, members may become disruptive, or apathetic, or even leave the group.

✦ Student Quotes

Different cultural and social backgrounds can be both beneficial and nonbeneficial. It depends on the maturity of the persons working together. If they respect each other, people from different backgrounds could really bring together some great ideas.

It is hard to be a leader when group members have cultural, philosophical, and political differences.

Leadership becomes challenging when the group is filled with people of differing backgrounds. It takes more effort to keep everyone working towards the same goal. The differences cause conflicts which must be resolved.

The differences allow greater adaptability and versatility for solving problems and communicating with other groups; however, they are an opportunity for conflict. Whether it is a good or bad thing depends on the surrounding circumstances.

Online Articles or Resources

- http://www.nytimes.com—In Students' Eyes, Look-Alike Lawyers Don't Make the Grade
- http://www.hbs.edu—Capitalizing on Diversity: Interpersonal Congruence in Small Work-Groups
- http://www.businessweek.com—Capitalizing on Diversity
- http://www.wkkf.org—Racial Equity
- http://www.nytimes.com—Companies Capitalizing on Worker Diversity
- www.nymbp.org/reference/WhitePrivilege.pdf—White Privilege by Peggy McIntosh
- www.diversitycentral.com/diversity_store/search.php —Resources for Cultural Diversity at Work

Suggested Books

- *Strengths-Based Leadership* by Tom Rath and Barry Conchie
- *Putting Our Differences to Work: The Fastest Way to Innovation, Leadership, and High Performance* by Debbe Kennedy and Joel A. Barker

- *Play to Your Strengths: Stacking the Deck to Achieve Spectacular Results for Yourself and Others* by Andrea Sigetich and Carol Leavitt
- *Paradigms: The Business of Discovering the Future* by Joel Arthur Barker
- *Five Regions of the Future: Preparing Your Business for Tomorrow's Technology Revolution* by Joel Arthur Barker and Scott Erickson
- *Making Diversity Work: Seven Steps for Defeating Bias in the Workplace* by Sondra Thiederman
- *Harvard Business Review on Managing Diversity* by R. Roosevelt Thomas, David A. Thomas, Robin J. Ely, and Debra Meyerson
- *The Difference: How the Power of Diversity Creates Better Groups, Firms, Schools, and Societies* by Scott E. Page

← Suggested Films

The following films highlight the capacity of capitalizing on difference. Some characters may overuse this capacity; others may lack the ability to use it successfully.

- *Remember the Titans*
- *Glory Road*
- *Lord of the Rings* trilogy
- *Star Wars* series
- *Harry Potter* series
- *Miracle*
- *Ocean's 11* and *12*
- *Milk*
- *Avatar*
- *X-Men*
- *Fantastic Four*
- *Glory*
- *The Blind Side*

↞ Potential Courses That Relate to This Capacity

- *Anthropology courses*—cultural anthropology
- *Business courses*—organizational behavior, leadership or management skills
- *Communication courses*—intercultural communication, small group communications, organizational communications
- *Leadership courses*
- *Psychology courses*—identity development, industrial and organizational psychology, social psychology
- *Sociology courses*—sociology of groups, community development

↞ Notable Quotes

We all live with the objective of being happy; our lives are all different and yet the same.—Anne Frank, author

Differences challenge assumptions.—Anne Wilson Schaef, author

For those who have seen the Earth from space, and for the hundreds and perhaps thousands more who will, the experience most certainly changes your perspective. The things that we share in our world are far more valuable than those which divide us.— Donald Williams, astronaut

As long as the differences and diversities of mankind exist, democracy must allow for compromise, for accommodation, and for the recognition of differences.—Eugene McCarthy, politician

The price of the democratic way of life is a growing appreciation of people's differences, not merely as tolerable, but as the essence of a rich and rewarding human experience.—Jerome Nathanson, journalist

We have become not a melting pot but a beautiful mosaic. Different people, different beliefs, different yearnings, different hopes, different dreams.—Jimmy Carter, thirty-ninth president of the United States of America

If we cannot end now our differences, at least we can help make the world safe for diversity.—John F. Kennedy, thirty-fifth president of the United States of America

← Reflection Questions

- In what ways might capitalizing on difference affect your organization's ability to stay relevant? (If you're not currently in an organization, think about another group you belong to.)
- Capitalizing on difference requires a certain mindset. What are some aspects of this way of thinking?
- What are the hallmarks of successfully leading a group with members who have differing world views, backgrounds, or mind-sets?

- What are your personal barriers when it comes to the capacity of capitalizing on difference?
- Think about a time when you were appreciated by a person or a group because you had a different point of view, idea, or set of skills. How did this make you feel? What do you believe were the results of your knowing that you were appreciated because of your difference?

Leadership is available to all of us. In fact, you do not need a formal title or position to lead others (think of Gandhi and Martin Luther King, Jr.). Sometimes you make a conscious decision to pursue a leadership role; other times the opportunity simply presents itself and you "step up." Either way, we agree with Joseph Rost (1993), who suggests that leadership is "an influence relationship among leaders and followers who intend real changes that reflect their mutual purposes" (p. 102). In other words, leaders and followers often collaborate toward a common end point. Each of us, often in a moment's notice, move from leader to follower depending on the context. So we suggest that leaders *and* followers can behave in an emotionally intelligent manner—it's not just about emotionally intelligent leadership, it's about emotionally intelligent followership as well.

Emotionally intelligent leadership asserts that an individual must be conscious of three fundamental facets that contribute to the leadership dynamic: consciousness of context, of self, and of others. These three facets overlap yet are independent of each other. Each facet consists of specific capacities that can be developed. A person's ability to monitor all three facets intentionally will enhance the person's ability to lead effectively.

Consciousness of Context

• *Environmental awareness:* Thinking intentionally about the environment of a leadership situation. The larger system, or environment, directly influences an individual's ability to lead. Aspects of the environment affect the psychological and interpersonal dynamics of any human interaction. Emotionally intelligent leaders are in tune with a variety of factors such as community traditions and customs, the political environment, and major institutions (e.g., religion, government).

• *Group savvy:* Interpreting the situation and/or networks of an organization. Every group has written/unwritten rules, ways of operating, customs and rituals, power dynamics, internal politics, inherent values and so forth. Emotionally intelligent leaders know how to diagnose and interpret these dynamics. Demonstrating group savvy enables one to have a direct influence on the work of the group.

Consciousness of Self

• *Emotional self-perception:* Identifying your emotions and reactions and their impact on you. Emotional self-perception means that individuals are acutely aware of their feelings (in real time). In addition, emotional self-perception means understanding how these feelings lead to behaviors. Having emotional self-perception also means that emotionally intelligent leaders have a choice as to how they respond. This capacity enables one to differentiate between the emotions felt and the actions taken. In most situations, both healthy and unhealthy responses are available.

• *Honest self-understanding:* Being aware of your own strengths and limitations. Honest self-understanding means that an individual celebrates and honors their strengths and talents while acknowledging and addressing limitations. Honest self-understanding means accepting the good and bad about one's personality, abilities, and ideas. When emotionally intelligent leaders demonstrate honest self-understanding, they embody a foundational capacity of effective leadership—the ability to see a more holistic self and understand how this impacts their leadership.

• *Healthy self-esteem:* Having a balanced sense of self. Emotionally intelligent leaders possess a high level of self-worth, are confident in their abilities, and are willing to stand up for what they believe in. They are also balanced by a sense of humility and the ability to create space for the opinions, perspectives, and thoughts of others.

- *Emotional self-control:* Consciously moderating your emotions and reactions. Although feeling emotions and being aware of them is part of this statement, so too is regulating them. Emotional self-control is about both awareness (being conscious of feelings) and action (managing emotions and knowing when and how to show them). Recognizing feelings, understanding how and when to demonstrate those feelings appropriately, and taking responsibility for one's emotions (versus being victims of them) are critical components of this capacity.

- *Authenticity:* Being transparent and trustworthy. Authenticity is a complex concept that emphasizes the importance of being trustworthy, transparent, and living in a way in which words match actions and vice versa. This is no small order. Being authentic means, in part, that emotionally intelligent leaders follow through on commitments and present themselves and their motives in an open and honest manner.

- *Flexibility:* Being open and adaptive to changing situations. The best laid plans don't always come to fruition, so emotionally intelligent leaders need to be responsive to change and open to feedback. By thinking creatively and using their problem-solving skills, emotionally intelligent leaders engage others in determining a new way to reach their goals.

- *Achievement:* Being driven to improve according to personal standards. An important nuance of this capacity is the role of personal standards. Individuals often know achievement when they see and feel it. Instead of letting others define what achievement looks like, emotionally intelligent leaders pursue their passions and goals to a self-determined level of accomplishment. This drive produces results and may inspire others to become more focused in their efforts or to work at increased levels as well.

- *Optimism:* Being positive. Emotionally intelligent leaders demonstrate a healthy, positive outlook and display a positive regard for the future. Optimism is a powerful force that many overlook. When demonstrated effectively, optimism is contagious and spreads throughout a group or organization.

- *Initiative:* Wanting and seeking opportunities. Emotionally intelligent leaders understand and take initiative. This means being assertive and seeking out opportunities. Emotionally intelligent leaders have to both see the opportunity for change and make it happen. Demonstrating initiative means that individuals take action and help the work of the group move forward.

Consciousness of Others

- *Empathy:* Understanding others from their perspective. Emotionally intelligent leadership and, more specifically, the capacity of empathy are about perceiving the emotions of others. When leaders display empathy, they have the opportunity to build healthier relationships, manage difficult situations, and develop trust more effectively. Being empathetic requires an individual to have a high level of self-awareness as well as awareness of others.

- *Citizenship:* Recognizing and fulfilling your responsibility for others or the group. Emotionally intelligent leaders must be aware of what it means to be a part of something bigger than themselves. An essential component is to fulfill the ethical and moral obligations inherent in the values of the community. As a result, emotionally intelligent leaders know when to give of themselves for the benefit of others and the larger group.

- *Inspiration:* Motivating and moving others toward a shared vision. Being perceived as an inspirational individual by others is an important capacity of emotionally intelligent leadership. Inspiration works through relationships. Effective leadership entails generating feelings of optimism and commitment to organizational goals through individual actions, words, and accomplishments.

• *Influence:* Demonstrating skills of persuasion. Emotionally intelligent leaders have the ability to persuade others with information, ideas, emotion, behavior, and a strong commitment to organizational values and purpose. They involve others to engage in a process of mutual exploration and action.

• *Coaching:* Helping others enhance their skills and abilities. Emotionally intelligent leaders know that they cannot do everything themselves. They need others to become a part of the endeavor. Coaching is about intentionally helping others demonstrate their talent and requires the emotionally intelligent leader to prioritize the time to foster the development of others in the group—not just themselves.

• *Change agent:* Seeking out and working with others toward new directions. As change agents, emotionally intelligent leaders look for opportunities for improvement or innovation—they think about possibilities and are future oriented. They see how change may benefit one person, an organization, or a whole community, and work to make this change happen.

• *Conflict management:* Identifying and resolving problems and issues with others. Emotionally intelligent leaders understand that conflict is part of any leadership experience. When managed effectively, conflict can foster great innovation. At times conflict is overt and may involve anger, raised voices, or high levels of frustration. Other times conflict is below the surface and shows itself only through cliques, side conversations, and apathy. Emotionally intelligent leaders are aware of these dynamics and work to manage them.

• *Developing relationships:* Creating connections between, among, and with people. Developing relationships is a skill as well as a mind-set. This capacity requires emotionally intelligent leaders to build relationships and create a sense of trust and mutual interest. Simply put, individuals, groups, and organizations are stronger, smarter, and more effective when they are rooted in and facilitate positive relationships.

- *Teamwork:* Working effectively with others in a group. Emotionally intelligent leaders know how to work with others to bring out the best in each team member. By facilitating good communication, creating shared purpose, clarifying roles, and facilitating results, emotionally intelligent leaders foster group cohesion and truly develop a sense of togetherness that leads to desired results.

- *Capitalizing on differences:* Building on assets that come from differences with others. Capitalizing on difference suggests that differences are seen as assets, not barriers. Difference may mean race, socio-economic status, religion, sexual orientation, or gender as well as ability, personality, or philosophy. When capitalized upon, these differences create a larger perspective—a more inclusive view. Emotionally intelligent leaders use these differences as an opportunity to help others grow, develop, and ultimately capitalize on them.

Where Emotional Intelligence and Student Leadership Unite

The book *Emotionally Intelligent Leadership* offers an in-depth explanation of the model and the tools for reflection on the concepts of leadership.

ISBN: 978-0-470-27713-3

Emotionally Intelligent Leadership for Students—Inventory offers a formative learning experience. The *Inventory* is an opportunity for individuals to explore their experiences in leadership with a focus on learning one's strengths and limitations based on past behaviors.

ISBN: 978-0-470-61572-0

Emotionally Intelligent Leadership for Students—Development Guide offers further guidance for development for each of the 21 capacities, including: definitions, student quotes, suggested experiences and activities, further reading and films to watch, notable quotes, and reflection questions.

ISBN: 978-0-470-61573-7

Emotionally Intelligent Leadership for Students—Workbook brings further understanding and relevancy to the EILS model. It includes modularized learning activities for each capacity, as well as some case studies, and resources for additional learning. It can be used as part of a facilitated course or workshop, or as a stand-alone, follow-up experience that students can use on their own.

ISBN: 978-0-470-61574-4

Emotionally Intelligent Leadership for Students—Facilitation and Activity Guide uses step-by-step instructions to lead facilitators and instructors through modularized activities found in the *EILS Workbook*. The modularized, timed activities can be taught out of sequence and customized to fit the needs of a curricular or co-curricular program. The guide offers various options and scenarios for using activities in different settings with different time constraints.

ISBN: 978-0-470-61575-1

SAVE ON SETS

Sets tailored for facilitators and students are available at discounted prices.
Visit www.josseybass.com for more information